WHAT OTHERS ARE SAYING ABOUT *reTHINK*

"After thirty-five years as a youth pastor (the past twenty-three in the same church), I will confess to you that I am not pleased with what we are "having." Thus, I need to take a hard look at what we're "doing." After reading *reThink* I see Steve "gets" it. His in-depth research and personal experiences come together to form a plan and model of what youth ministry must look like if we are to turn the tides within the church in reaching and keeping youth. I'd buy the book just for chapter one! It is must reading for anyone involved in making a difference in this world by investing their life into the lives of teenagers."

PHIL NEWBERRY
STUDENT PASTOR, BELLEVUE BAPTIST CHURCH, CORDOVA, TENNESSEE

"In a time where we are literally fighting for the souls of teenagers, Steve Wright is bringing a refreshing look at what it takes to do kingdom student ministry. Steve has been a personal friend of mine in student ministry for the last eight years. Steve has a veteran's point of view of student ministry, which he personally practices in his student ministry at Providence. The book *reThink* will definitely make you rethink the why's and how's of student ministry. I couldn't recommend a better book when it comes to shaping students heading into the future."

CHRIS D. LOVELL
MINISTER TO STUDENTS, PRESTONWOOD BAPTIST CHURCH, PLANO, TEXAS

"I'm getting a copy of *reThink* for EVERY parent in my ministry."

CHRIS SWAN
STUDENT PASTOR, LAWNDALE BAPTIST CHURCH, GREENSBORO, NORTH CAROLINA

"I believe Steve Wright has hit a nerve! We must realize that the current model of student ministry that emphasizes the separation of students from parents is doomed for failure. *reThink* is one of the most relevant books I've read in years!"

CALVIN J. CARR
HIGH SCHOOL PASTOR, FIRST BAPTIST JACKSONVILLE, FLORIDA

"As churches try to solve the mystery of declining long-term impact of the church in the lives of students, one sacred cow has been left alone in the search...the standard way student ministry has operated over the past few decades. Steve Wright has been willing to step out of line and take an honest look at the biblical principles involved in ministry to students. The results are refreshing as he has blazed a trail into new (or actually age-old) directions for leading students to know, love, and serve Christ. This book offers a challenging model for student ministry that is now bearing fruit in our own congregation. I cannot tell you how excited I am about what the Lord is doing through this biblical approach to reaching students for Christ!"

DAVID HORNER
SENIOR PASTOR, PROVIDENCE BAPTIST CHURCH, RALEIGH, NORTH CAROLINA

"Over the past several years Steve has helped me gain a fresh perspective on what it means to come alongside parents and co-champion a student's faith."

SHAWN SMITH
STUDENT PASTOR, FIRST BAPTIST SPRINGDALE, ARKANSAS

"Thank you Steve for the WAKE UP CALL! This book is a must read for all pastors, parents, and student leaders. We plan to make it available for all of our families."

SHONN KEELS
SENIOR PASTOR, CAROLINA FOREST COMMUNITY CHURCH, MYRTLE BEACH, SOUTH CAROLINA

"A lot has been said in recent years about the need for more family-based student ministry, and while many agree, change has been slow in coming. However, Steve Wright, with his fresh and welcomed approach—tried and tested in the laboratory of a thriving student ministry which he leads—is providing the formula."

VICTOR FLORES
PASTOR OF STUDENT MINISTRIES, BELL SHOALS BAPTIST CHURCH, BRANDON, FLORIDA

"For years, the church has bought into the lie that children do not listen to or respect their parents, or that the church in two or three hours a week can have a greater spiritual impact on children/teenagers than the parents who impact their students for hours on end each week. Steve and Tina Wright have successfully reminded and modeled that the parents ARE the most effective disciplers of their children."

SCOTT HEATH
STUDENT MINISTER, SHADES MOUNTAIN BAPTIST CHURCH, BIRMINGHAM, ALABAMA

"Steve Wright has expanded my understanding of my call as a student pastor. He has helped me understand that part of my call is to come alongside parents and help them do what they are called to do, which is to disciple their children."

TRENT PEACOCK
STUDENT PASTOR, HICKORY GROVE BAPTIST CHURCH, CHARLOTTE, NORTH CAROLINA

"Steve Wright has insight into parent ministry that is born out of being a parent himself plus almost twenty years of student ministry experience. He has captured some unique insights and approaches to parent ministry that can help you get a handle on this illusive and sometimes frustrating ministry. His love for parents and their students has been the key motivating factor, and I think you will find it on most of the pages of *reThink*."

RANDY JOHNSON
MINISTER OF YOUTH EDUCATION, FIRST BAPTIST CHURCH RICHARDSON, TEXAS

reTHiNK

DECiDE FOR YOURSELF

reTHiNK

iS STUDENT MiNiSTRY WORKiNG?

STeve WRiGHT

WiTH CHRis GRaves

INQUEST PUBLISHING

reThink

Copyright © 2008 by InQuest Publishing

Published by InQuest Publishing, P.O. Box 2055, Wake Forest, NC 27588
For general information, call 1-800-776-1893 • 919-453-0116
E-Mail: info@inquest.org • http://www.inquest.org

ISBN 978-1-931548-69-4

Cover design and layout by LeAnn Gentry

ISBN
Printed in the United States of America
2007—First Edition
2008—Second Edition

THIS BOOK IS DEDICATED TO PARENTS PAST, PRESENT, AND FUTURE:

My parents—Thank you for beginning a legacy of faith that has changed my life and many others. I pray that I can model the principles in this book as consistently as you have.

My wife—Tina—I am blessed to walk through this life each day with you. Thank you for your endless encouragement and love.

My children—Sara, William, and Tyler—You each inspire me and bring untold joy and laughter. I pray God continues a lasting legacy for our family through each of you.

TABLE OF CONTENTS

FORWARD

Those of us who love teenagers and sense a clear call from God to serve in this critical area of life have heard the horror stories of the ineffectiveness of today's youth ministries. Some of the criticism is justified and some is not. In spite of the many wonderful youth ministries spanning our country/world, most research reveals that at least 50 percent of active evangelical teenagers leave church between ages eighteen and twenty-one, and few of those ever return. It is apparent that some adjusting and retooling of today's approaches to youth ministry are in order.

reThink challenges those who are called to youth ministry to rethink not just practical youth ministry but the philosophy that drives why and how we do youth ministry. Having served in full-time youth ministry for more than 30 years and teaching youth ministry courses at Southwestern Baptist Theological Seminary since fall of 2004, I have read a multitude of wonderful books on the subject. With all honesty and sincerity, *reThink* is the most valuable book on youth ministry I have read up to this point in my career.

I have known Steve Wright as a personal friend for many years and have observed him in nearly every aspect of ministry. He writes as he lives. The philosophy and concepts discussed are what he has put into practice in his ministry and not mere ideas that have been tossed about in late-night discussions. With every aspect of culture, media and the educational system pulling at today's youth, a critical book is needed for these critical times. *reThink* is that book.

Johnny L. Derouen, Ph.D.
Southwestern Baptist Theological Seminary
Fort Worth, TX

INTRODUCTION

How's your ministry going? No, really. How's your ministry, your calling, your life going?

We are all aware of our calling to build disciples and to reach this generation, but we also are called to minister to our families, our wives, and our kids, as well as to keep our personal walks strong. So, how's it going? Are you really satisfied with the direction of your ministry and your life? Is this what you pictured student ministry would be like?

My name is Steve Wright. I have been a student pastor for more than twenty years, and if the Lord allows I hope to be in student ministry for many years to come. My co-author is Chris Graves, who has just begun his second decade as a student pastor and also hopes to continue for years to come. We're not some supposed outside experts looking in on student ministry. We know what student ministry is like because it is what we do every day. We've been blessed and burned, encouraged one minute and discouraged the next. We've lain awake at night wrestling with the same questions you have: "Is my ministry really effective?" and "Is all this really impacting eternity?"

We often talk to student pastors and ask them how life is going, really going. I've spoken with well over a thousand student pastors, and every one I've met moves at Mach 3. We're all busy doing ministry: planning events, preparing lessons, praying for direction, counseling teens and parents, trying to reach teens in their world, leading our families, and trying to maintain a full spiritual life so that we can minister out of the overflow. Many of you are also busy attending and finishing school or working a second job to allow you to minister. We are all busy, so busy trying to keep up with ministry that we often don't have time to pull back, take an honest evaluation, and answer the tough questions that linger in the back of our minds. This book is about those hard questions.

Let me invite you to be real with us and to be honest for once about student ministry and your life. I know the questions you wrestle with because I have wrestled with the same ones. I have had the same doubts and thought that maybe I was the problem; "Maybe I just can't make it in ministry." I've questioned, "Is this worth giving my life for?" I've wondered if I needed another degree. I've thought that maybe I just need to do more, work harder, or start a new program and maybe then I would find soul satisfaction. Those aren't the answers because we're asking the wrong questions. The better questions, which this book will answer, are: Why are so many guys in the trenches facing the same problems? Why are the majority of teens leaving the faith after graduation? Why are many leaving this profession after such a short stay? And, what does the Bible teach about how the family and the church are supposed to truly partner together?

This book was born out of deciding to rethink student ministry. We started by asking some tough questions, searching the Bible for its framework for ministry, looking at the latest research, and being honest about the problems of student ministry. Our prayer is that these pages encourage you because we know how hard student pastors work and how passionately they care about this generation. We know that it is hard to find the time to pull back from a frantic ministry lifestyle and honestly evaluate where student ministry is heading. We challenge you to be honest. Approach the research and Bible study in these pages with an open mind and some critical thinking and decide for yourself if student ministry is accomplishing what everyone thinks it is. If it is producing lasting results in our students and soul satisfaction in our personal and family lives, then let's continue doing what we are doing. But if it isn't, and I believe it isn't, it's time for a change.

It's time for us to be honest about our struggles and frantic lifestyles. It's time to admit that the current student ministry model isn't aligned with a biblical framework. It's time to be honest about what today's research is telling us. It's time to rethink student ministry.

reSEarcH:

Gauging Student

Ministry Today

"Houston, we have a problem." On April 14, 1970, Jim Lovell radioed those ominous words from the *Apollo 13* spacecraft to the command center in Houston, Texas. Lovell and the rest of the crew knew that something was wrong but were slowly learning the extent of the problem. The command center in Houston first assumed the gauges had to be mistaken. The team finally determined the gauges weren't wrong; the number two oxygen tank had exploded and critically damaged several parts of the spacecraft, leaving them with little oxygen and little power. Making matters worse, the spacecraft was more than 199,000 miles from earth. Gene Kranz, the flight director for the mission, said, "Every controller stared incredulously at his display and reported new pieces to add to the puzzle. Because we thought the problems were caused by an electrical glitch, I believed we would quickly nail the problem and get back on track. It was fifteen minutes before we began to comprehend the full scope of the crisis. Once we understood it, we realized that there was not going to be a lunar mission. The mission had become one of survival."[1]

It seems that most student pastors are tapping their knuckles on the gauges, thinking surely the gauges must be wrong. They are not wrong, and if we do not change course, our mission will fail.

Today, our mission as student pastors is at a critical point, but you would never know it by watching some churches. Our methods have stayed the same while the statistics are becoming ominous. Students are leaving the church at an alarming rate. Student pastors are walking away from ministry. Fewer students are being reached for Christ and baptized. Fewer Christian teens have a basic understanding of the Bible. Our mission is becoming one of survival, but our ministry model isn't changing accordingly. "It seems that most student pastors are tapping their knuckles on the gauges, thinking surely the gauges must be wrong. They are not wrong, and if we do not change course, our mission will fail."

I recently turned forty-one, and I have been blessed to serve the local church in student ministry for over twenty years. My wife, Tina, and I have three children, all currently in my student ministry. I am at a place in my life where I must ask some tough questions and confront some brutal facts. This topic is more than a lighthearted debate about methodology to me. Students' souls are at stake, including three in my own family. I passionately believe that it's time to reexamine what we are doing as student pastors.

When I began as a student pastor, I inherited a model of student ministry that I assumed was biblically based and time tested. I would plan hard, pray harder, train leaders, and hope for the best. One of my mentors often reminded me that the effectiveness of my student ministry may not be seen until five years after someone has graduated from my ministry. His words, along with John 15:16, rang in my ears reminding me that the goal is to produce "fruit that will last." I still believe his logic is correct, but I never questioned the accepted model of student ministry and never had a way to quantify the long-term results that model produced. Today's research provides the results we've needed for some time.

So, what are the gauges that allow you and me to test the effectiveness of our current model of student ministry? I believe that at least four gauges tell us we have a problem.

They are:
- Student retention rates
- Student pastor tenures
- Student baptism rates
- Student Bible literacy

There are other gauges we could and should monitor, but these four are clear indicators of how we are doing. The results are now in. Read the facts. Decide for yourself. Is the current model of student ministry accomplishing what we assumed it would? If it is working, then great; let's not change a thing. However, if the gauges are indicating what I think they are, then our mission is in serious danger, and we must change the course.

GAUGE ONE:
STUDENT RETENTION RATES

I have often heard that every organization and every person must ask himself two questions: "What business are you in?" and "How's business?"[2] We are in the business of reaching students with the gospel and discipling them into fully committed followers of Christ. Our business is that of equipping students to walk with Christ not just during their teen years but for a lifetime. So, how's business? Is the church reproducing itself in young people who are passionate for Christ and the church? Recently, we have begun to see the research become clear in the area of student retention. Here is what the research says:

- A recent *TIME* Magazine article points to research which found that 61 percent of the adults polled who are now in their twenties said they had participated in church activities as teens but no longer do. Some argue that young people typically drift from organized religion in early adulthood, but others say the high attrition is a sign that churches need to change the way they try to engage the next generation.[3]

- A study from UCLA found that almost half of college students drift away from their Christian upbringing. While 52 percent of incoming students said that they regularly took part in church events, the number shrinks to 29 percent who are still involved in church activities by their junior year.[4]

- Josh McDowell estimates, "Over 69 percent of youth are leaving traditional church after high school."[5]

- LifeWay Christian Research reports, "The overwhelming majority of children from evangelical families are leaving the church as they enter adulthood."[6]

- Mark Matlock finds, "Depending on whose numbers you use, 58 percent-84 percent of graduating youth from church youth groups are not returning."[7]

- David Wheaton, author of *University of Destruction*, states that "as many as 50 percent of Christian students say they have lost their faith after four years of college."[8]

- George Barna gives troubling news in his book *Real Teens*: "Now only 33 percent of churched youth say that the church will play a part in their lives when they leave home."[9]

- Glenn Schultz at LifeWay Christian Resources estimates that 75 percent of young people leave church in their late teens and aren't reconnecting later.[10]

- Student Venture reports that about 70 percent of seniors in high school who claimed faith stop attending church during the college years.[11]

- Ron Luce in *Battle Cry for a Generation* estimates "88 percent of kids raised in Christian homes do not continue to follow the Lord after they graduate from high school."[12]

- LifeWay Research found that 70 percent of young adults ages twenty-three to thirty stopped attending church regularly for at least a year between the ages of eighteen and twenty-two. They also found that 20 percent more of those who did not leave the church had a family member who talked to them about spiritual things.[13]

- *USA Today* reported on the same LifeWay research as above. However, they said that the news wasn't "all bad." Thirty-five percent of those who dropped out of church started coming back by the age of thirty. It is a sad day when churches comfort themselves with the fact that around one-third of drop outs later return, which still means around two-thirds leave the church for good after student ministry.[14]

Who would have ever imagined that through the accumulation of the abundance of ministry tools available to us today that our effectiveness might be diminishing? As a student ministry staff, we have discussed how revealing it would be if we had two hundred of our middle school students stand and then asked 70-75 percent of them to sit down to represent those who would walk away from the church after graduation. That's a sobering thought, especially remembering that two of my own children are in our middle school ministry. Imagine what that would look like in your church.

No statistic tells the entire story. I am sure that the percentages given above vary greatly depending on one's region, denomination, church health, or ministry context. While it is true that percentages may vary, I have spoken with numerous seminary professors, student pastors, denominational leaders, and senior pastors, and every one of them is very concerned with the upward trend of students leaving the church. Let me encourage you to read through the above statistics once more and contrast it with what Jesus said about this very issue in Luke 15:4-6:

> Suppose one of you has a hundred sheep and loses one of them. Does he not leave the ninety-nine in the open country and go after the lost sheep until he finds it? And when he finds it, he joyfully puts it on his shoulders and goes home. Then he calls his friends and neighbors together and says, "Rejoice with me; I have found my lost sheep."

When we consider the investment that has been made in the lives of this generation of students, it is difficult to believe how many students are leaving evangelical churches and their faith. The investment begins much sooner than youth ministry. Children are placed in church nurseries at birth, and then they move into exciting children's ministries that encourage their faith development. The next few years are spent in middle school ministries, which include weekend trips, concerts with Christian celebrities, lock-ins, and Bible studies geared for their ages. The same students move into high school ministries with weeklong camps, mission trips, leadership retreats, choirs, discipleship classes, Wednesday night youth groups, Sunday morning Bible classes, and the list goes on and on. The church makes a huge investment by providing professional staff, youth ministry budgets, enhanced youth rooms, and sometimes buildings with the latest technology. With all the time, money, and energy poured into teens, why are we not getting a better return for our investment?

> With all the time, money, and energy poured into teens, why are we not getting a better return for our investment?

Dr. Alvin Reid addresses student retention rates in his book *Raising the Bar*, when he states, "It is obvious that youth ministry in America has not produced a generation of young people who are passionate about the church."[15] He goes on to explain that of the hundreds of student pastors with whom he meets nationally, many recognize the need for reformation of youth ministry, yet most have more questions than answers.[16]

GAUGE TWO:
STUDENT PASTOR TENURES

"And as for you, brothers, never tire of doing what is right" (2 Thessalonians 3:13). It is common knowledge, and sometimes the fuel for jokes, that student pastors stay at a church for a short time, change churches often, and sometimes quit the vocation altogether after a few years in the ministry. Churches of all sizes constantly struggle to keep this position filled. One would think with the countless youth ministry degree programs in our schools that prepare student pastors, not to mention the conferences, books, seminars, retreats, and other opportunities for continued training, that student pastors would survive longer than a few years in ministry. Why is there such a high turnover rate among student pastors? Factors that contribute to the turnover rates can clearly be seen in a study conducted by Associations of Youth Ministry Educators:

> While this study seems to dismiss the much quoted
> 18-month tenure of youth ministers, it shows that many
> change churches after only a few years. The reasons for
> leaving a church include inadequate salaries, greater
> opportunities for successful work in a new position,
> conflict with senior pastors, unhealthy spiritual environ-
> ment within the church, and disillusionment with their
> present local church. This study also shows that many
> have short careers in the vocation. *These findings seem
> to confirm that youth ministry does not attract many in-*

dividuals for the long haul. A possible reason for these tenure patterns may be due to the young age at which these participants entered youth ministry.

This interdenominational study conducted by Associations of Youth Ministry Educators included current and former youth ministers in the U.S. who were members of the National Network of Youth Ministries. The following question was asked in this study: What are the tenure patterns of current and former youth ministers?

Age Began as Youth Ministers. The majority of all participants (63.0%) began work as youth ministers before the age of 25, with the most frequent age being 21. Current and former youth ministers were very similar in their responses related to this item.

Length of Tenure in Youth Minister Positions. The mean length of tenure in a youth minister position of all participants was 4.7 years, and the median was 3.1 years. Among participants, 15.6% averaged less than two years in a youth minister position. 8.4% of all participants averaged more than 10 years in a youth minister position.

Age Former Youth Ministers Left the Vocation. The majority (56.9%) of former youth ministers were in their thirties when they left the vocation, with the second largest group (21.5%) leaving during their twenties. There were four common influential factors identified by both current and former youth ministers.

1. *Salary/benefits inadequate.* Many reported that their salary and/or benefits were inadequate. Some stated that they had not received a cost-of-living increase in years.

2. *Disillusionment with this local church.* Many felt they had become discouraged by the general direction or effectiveness of their former church. This created a difficult climate in which to work.

3. *Greater opportunity for successful work in my new position.* Though this factor could be related to various issues (i.e., relationships, support, vision, and finance), many believed that they could be more successful in a different ministry context or career.

4. *Personal needs going unmet.* Both current and former youth ministers reported that their personal needs were going unmet at their former ministry context or in the vocation.[17]

When I first received this research from the Association of Youth Ministry Educators, one bit of information was especially troubling. They asked those who had left youth ministry, "How has the change of church employer or leaving youth ministry affected the life of current and former youth ministers?" While most reported an improvement in all twenty-one areas asked about, there was a significant improvement in four areas: relationship with God, view of the local church, relationship with co-workers, and financial situation.[18] Of those four areas which improved, the first one was the most alarming. Most of those surveyed reported that their relationship with God improved once they left youth ministry. Maybe that isn't so surprising; maybe we have come to accept a model of youth ministry that isn't spiritually healthy for those who lead it or for their families. When I look at these numbers, I do not have the luxury of being an outsider looking in on the problem. Student ministry is what I do, and as far as I know it will be what I do until I die. My supervising pastor often reminds me, "When we do God's work God's way, then our lives should be marked with a badge of distinction"—namely soul rest, soul satisfaction, and soul sufficiency.[19] When student pastors' lives are not marked by these traits, it makes me wonder if we assumed a responsibility that wasn't biblically assigned.

Throughout its brief history, the vocation of student ministry has been plagued with a reputation for high stress, low status, inadequate pay, high job expectations, poor pastoral staff relationships, and high staff turnover. One researcher summarized the problems for youth ministers in the Roman Catholic Church and likely those in Protestant churches as well:

> Of the various ministry positions, youth ministers seem to derive the least satisfaction and support. The full-time youth ministers find ministry the least affirming, their co-workers the least affirming, their supervisors the least satisfied, parishioners the least satisfied, and youth ministers the least likely to encourage others to enter parish ministry.[20]

Let's face it; student ministry isn't for the faint of heart. I can't begin to recall all the conversations I have had with student pastors who were wounded, discouraged, beat up emotionally, about to resign, or be let go. I can honestly tell you that I have had my moments of great discouragement before I reminded myself of Whom I serve and my calling to ministry. What student pastor do you know who hasn't had these days?

Think of the effects of short student pastor tenures. Very few student pastors serve long enough at one church to see a student go through an entire student ministry from beginning to end. Churches must seriously consider this issue since students often model what they see in their leaders. If this problem isn't addressed, then a generation of students will likely conclude that being part of a church body doesn't require long-term commitment as they have seen their leaders come and go. I recently had a conversation with a college student who shared with me that he had four different student pastors in the church where he grew up.

When I am asked how we developed a seven-year curriculum map[21] for our students, I always respond by saying it started with the realization that my family and I would be here that long. The church, our students, our student pastors, and their families would be much healthier with a longer-lasting relationship. While this may require both student pastors and church leaders to have some very open and honest conversations, the church should take note of the revolving door of student pastors and the example it sets for our students.

GAUGE THREE:
STUDENT BAPTISM RATES

"How many did your church baptize last year?" Those who are into the numbers game often toss around that question, while others cringe and remind them that it's not all about numbers. That's very true; baptism numbers don't come close to telling the whole story. But, before we are too quick to dismiss them, baptism rates are a clear and widely accepted gauge of our effectiveness to penetrate our culture and reach people for Christ. Maybe one reason student pastors avoid the numbers' talk is that baptism rates are declining. Reid observes:

> Over the preceding twenty years the number of full-time youth pastors has grown dramatically and a plethora of magazines, music, and ideas aimed at youth had been birthed along the way. Meanwhile, during that same time span, the numbers of young people won to Christ dropped at about as fast a rate.

He concludes by saying, "If we keep doing what we're doing, we'll keep getting what we're getting!"[22]

Last year more than 23,000 Southern Baptist churches (SBC) baptized no teens. Thom Rainer states that "82 percent of all Southern Baptist churches baptized twelve or less persons during 2003." He concludes, "Frankly, most Southern Baptist churches today are evangelistically anemic. The bulk of baptisms in the denomination are taking place in a relatively few

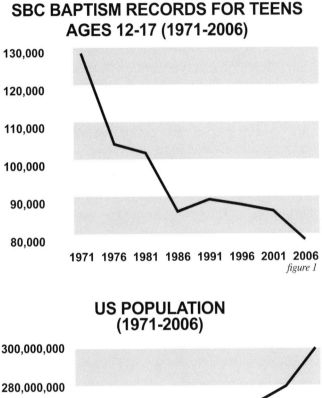

SBC BAPTISM RECORDS FOR TEENS AGES 12-17 (1971-2006)

figure 1

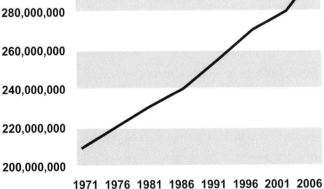

US POPULATION (1971-2006)

figure 2

churches."[23] During the past thirty years, SBC baptisms have declined. There were 1,346,597 total baptisms from 1976 to 1990 and 1,259,560 from 1991 to 2005. This equals 87,019 fewer baptisms over the previous fifteen years.[24]

Baptisms as a whole have declined, but they have declined even more sharply for students ages twelve to seventeen (see Figure 1). This is not a Southern Baptist problem alone. *USA Today* recently published an article alarmingly titled "The Rite of Baptism Trickles Away." In it the author states, "Methodists and Lutherans have seen both baptisms and their membership numbers slide for years. Even... the Assemblies of God, which has had a boom in membership since 1980, saw its annual baptism numbers peak in 1997, then inch downward."[25] It seems that churches of all denominations and sizes are failing to reach teens with the gospel and baptize them.

It's very difficult to explain this decline when you examine the efforts churches are making to reach students: age-specific resources, technology, youth buildings, larger budgets, weekend conferences, additional support staff, more churches, events with Christian celebrities, and other youth events designed to reach unchurched teenagers. Many of these efforts have actually supported and led many students to Christ throughout the years, so these tools, resources, and efforts obviously are not the problem. Most churches are making great strides to reach this generation, and parents and families must do the same. Perhaps the reason student pastors aren't reaching more teens is because the task was never exclusively biblically assigned to them. Perhaps what is needed is not another packaged youth ministry evangelism program but rather a biblical burden. It kind of makes you wonder how churches were so successful in the 1950s when baptism numbers soared and there were no catalogs full of clever programs. Greg Stier gives us a better place to look for youth ministry wisdom by reminding us, "We have within the pages of Scripture everything we need to truly be successful in youth ministry."[26]

Thom Rainer says it like this: "Courses in youth ministry should prepare men and women to evangelize the age segment (teens). We have sorely neglected this group too long. It is time to reconsider youth ministry."[27] Sadly many student pastors are told that the solution to the declining conversions is to work harder or do ministry bigger and better. But, if our programs are bigger, our budgets are bigger, our shows are bigger, and our workloads as pastors are bigger, then why are baptisms still declining? The solution isn't to kick the traditional student ministry model up a notch; the solution is to reexamine how the Bible should guide our framework to develop students and encourage the parents and adults who influence them.

> But, if our programs are bigger, our budgets are bigger, our shows are bigger, and our workloads as pastors are bigger, then why are baptisms still declining?

Figure 1 is even more revealing when you balance today's baptism rates against the U.S. population of more than three hundred million and the fact that it has almost grown by one hundred million since the early 1970s (see Figure 2). If the population is growing and the size of our student ministry events are growing but baptisms are falling, then we must rethink how we do youth ministry.

GAUGE FOUR:
STUDENT BIBLE LITERACY

The final gauge tells us how effectively we are educating our students. Are our students being prepared to articulate and defend their faith in a gentle and attractive manner? First Peter 3:15-16 speaks of this preparedness:

> But in your hearts set apart Christ as Lord. Always be prepared to give an answer to everyone who asks you to give the reason for the hope that you have. But do this with gentleness and respect, keeping a clear conscience, so that those who speak maliciously against your good behavior in Christ may be ashamed of their slander.

The Bible is clear that every Christian's task, including the teenagers in our ministries, is to be ready to give biblical answers and defend the faith. With today's multicultural society where our students face different beliefs daily, it is more important than ever that students know and are able to articulate what they believe. I understand this passage isn't saying that teens must have an answer for every obscure or ridiculous question, but I believe they should have a strong, solid understanding of the foundational truths of God's Word. So, are our students equipped to explain these basic truths to another person? Do they possess a basic biblical worldview? Unfortunately, the gauge indicates that fewer students today are biblically literate.

The Nehemiah Institute in Lexington, Kentucky, researched more than 15,000 students in various Christian schools by conducting a worldview-testing program known as PEERS Testing. This test evaluates an individual's belief in five major areas of life: politics, economics, education, religion, and social issues (PEERS). Views in each category are identified as belonging to one of four major worldview philosophies: 1) biblical theism, 2) moderate Christianity, 3) secular humanism, or 4) socialism. The research suggests that 85 percent of youth from Christian homes who attend public schools do not embrace a biblical worldview. While students in Christian schools scored slightly higher than their public school counterparts, only 6 percent of students embraced the biblical theism worldview.[28]

Our culture is mass broadcasting a worldview very different than the one in the Bible. How is the world distorting our teens' views about Christianity? Barna Research Group provides more statistics showing how the teens' beliefs today differ from those of their parents.

- Sixty-three percent don't believe Jesus is the Son of the one true God.
- Fifty-eight percent believe all faiths teach equally valid truths.
- Fifty-one percent don't believe Jesus rose from the dead.
- Sixty-five percent don't believe Satan is a real entity.
- Sixty-eight percent don't believe the Holy Spirit is a real entity.

In another study of teenagers, of which 70 percent were active in church youth group and 82 percent identified themselves as Christians, Barna found:

- Sixty-three percent believe Muslims, Buddhists, Christians, Jews, and all other people pray to the same god, even though they use different names for their god.
- Eighty-seven percent of our kids believe Jesus was a real person who came to earth, and 78 percent believe He was born of a virgin, yet nearly half (46 percent) believe He committed sins and over half (51 percent) say He died but did not rise from the dead.
- Fifty-eight percent believe that all religious faiths teach equally valid truth.[29]

Newsweek and Beliefnet.com asked 1,004 Americans this question: "Can a good person who doesn't share your religious beliefs attain salvation or go to heaven?" Sixty-eight percent of evangelical Protestants said yes.[30]

It's hard to read facts like these and not go into statistic overload. The basis of these statistics is explained well by Josh McDowell: "It's not that they haven't embraced a version of Christianity; it's simply that the version they believe in is not built on the true foundation of what biblical Christianity is all about."[31]

Christian Smith in his groundbreaking national research says,

It seems to us that religious educators need to work much harder on articulation. We were astounded by the realization that for very many teens we interviewed, it seemed as if our interview was the first time any adult had ever asked them what they believed. By contrast, the same teens could be remarkably articulate about other subjects about which they had been drilled, such as drinking, drugs, STDs and safe sex. It was also astonishing how many Christian teens, for example, were comfortable talking generally about God but not specifically about Jesus.[32]

Smith also says,

Scholars who have looked at young Christians say their spiritual drift is in part the result of a lack of knowledge about their faith. The vast majority of teens who call themselves Christians haven't been well educated in religious doctrine and therefore really don't know what they believe.[33]

Let me be clear: I am not blaming student pastors. The research isn't saying that we aren't working hard enough or that we aren't smart enough to teach the Bible well. The facts show that the opposite is true; the majority of student pastors work hard and do all they can for students. The model of student ministry that we have inherited and embraced has led us to where we are now. I believe that these statistics are products of churches and parents misunderstanding their biblically assigned duties. Therefore, we must decide if it is time to reexamine the model in which student pastors and parents teach biblical truth.

WHAT THE GAUGES MEAN

Why is it so crucial for us to be aware of these four gauges? I'm not saying that numbers are all-important or that we need to double-up our efforts to make these numbers look better. These numbers are simply gauges, like those on the *Apollo 13* spacecraft, that tell us where we are headed and if there's a problem. These four gauges point to a hard fact—our mission is in trouble. The mission we are on has two goals: to glorify God and to build His kingdom. These gauges tell us that we're not fulfilling our mission as well as we thought.

Think about Hebrews 3:12-14:

See to it, brothers, that none of you has a sinful, unbelieving heart *that turns away from the living God.* But encourage one another daily, as long as it is called

today, so that none of you may be hardened by sin's
deceitfulness.

Also think of John 15:10-11:

If you obey my commands, you will *remain in my
love,* just as I have obeyed my Father's commands and
remain in his love. I have told you this so that my joy
may be in you and that your joy may be complete.

Unfortunately, Gauge 1 tells us that a majority of the
teens in our ministries are turning from the living God after graduation. The goal isn't successful programs, events,
or models, but that everyone remains in Christ and becomes
complete in Him. Today's model is failing in those tasks a
majority of the time. Acts 20:28-31 tells us:

Keep watch over yourselves and all the flock of which
the Holy Spirit has made you overseers. Be shepherds
of the church of God, which he bought with his own
blood. I know that after I leave, savage wolves will
come in among you and will not spare the flock. Even
from your own number men will arise and distort the
truth in order to draw away disciples after them. So be
on your guard!

As we saw in Gauge 2, student pastors are leaving in
record numbers and are abandoning the flock God entrusted
to them. It intrigues me that the first command of the above
passage is to watch yourselves, and the research clearly

shows that student pastors aren't doing so, as their spiritual, family, and personal lives suffer in today's student ministry model. The goal is not to spend a specific number of years in ministry but to become a shepherd who loves God's flock and God's church. In Acts 2:38-40 we read:

> Peter replied, "Repent and be baptized, every one of you, in the name of Jesus Christ for the forgiveness of your sins. And you will receive the gift of the Holy Spirit. The promise is for you and your children and for all who are far off—for all whom the Lord our God will call." With many other words he warned them; and he pleaded with them, "Save yourselves from this corrupt generation."

Baptism has from the first day of the church been a key part of a person's Christian experience, but according to Gauge 3 it is becoming less common. Instead of seeing baptism's significance increase, we see our teens becoming corrupted by the generation they should be impacting for Christ. Our end goal is not to baptize more than we did thirty years ago but to produce disciples who impact the world for Christ. Finally, 1 Corinthians 8:2-3 exhorts us by saying:

> We know that we all possess knowledge. Knowledge puffs up, but love builds up. The man who thinks he knows something does not yet know as he ought to know. But the man who loves God is known by God.

Gauge 4 reminds us that our students aren't being

equipped with knowledge of the Lord, His Word, and His ways. I love the 1 Corinthians 8 passage because it teaches us that our goal is to produce not smarter sinners but rather Christ followers whose knowledge leads to a greater love for God.

A hard look at these four gauges may not be pleasant, but it is necessary for those who serve the church and its important mission to reach this generation. A couple of organizations have conducted studies that show the importance of student ministry in the life of local church congregations. The American Institute for Church Growth found that "ministry to youth was the second most important reason people give for joining a congregation in their study." Group Publishing surveyed 553 families in twenty rapidly growing churches to identify what attracts them to a specific church. For these families, preaching ranked first in importance and youth ministry ranked second.[34] Church leaders have long noted the importance of both children's and youth ministries as priorities for attracting families in their communities. Abandoning student ministry is not the answer.

While many churches and church leaders realize the importance of student ministry within the life of the church body, they are rightly concerned with the problems these gauges are revealing. If the church is not able to keep its youth or those called to reach and equip them and if the church isn't effectively reaching and equipping students to defend their faith, then we can easily see that we are in the middle of a major crisis. A recent article in *TIME* Magazine states the frustration of many student pastors:

> Youth ministers have been on a long and frustrating quest of their own over the past two decades or so. Believing that a message wrapped in pop-culture packaging was the way to attract teens to their flocks, pastors watered down the religious content and boosted the entertainment. But in recent years churches have begun offering their young people a style of religious instruction grounded in Bible study and teachings about the doctrines of their denomination. Their conversion has been sparked by the recognition that sugarcoated Christianity, popular in the 1980s and early '90s, has caused growing numbers of kids to turn away not just from attending youth-fellowship activities but also from practicing their faith at all.[35]

When the *Apollo 13* spacecraft was 199,000 miles from earth, the crew's mission changed. The change began when the crew and flight controllers in Houston started believing their gauges. They wasted no time, gathered the facts, made the needed changes, and saved lives. The parallels are easy to see. Our gauges – student retention rates, student pastor tenures, student baptism rates, and student literacy of the Bible – are telling us that our mission is at a critical point. Like those in the *Apollo 13* mission, we must begin to find solutions. Church, we have a problem.

NOTES

1 Gene Kranz, *Failure Is Not an Option* (New York, NY: A Berkley Book, 2001), p.311.

2 My thanks to Chris Swan for often asking these two questions.

3 Sonja Steptoe/Bellflower, "In Touch with Jesus", *Time* Magazine, October 31, 2006.

4 Taken from abcnews.go.com/GMA/story?id=1375842&page=1.

5 Josh McDowell, *The Last Christian Generation* (Holiday, FL: Green Key Books, 2006), p.13.

6 "Lord, Send Your Holy Spirit," SBC Annual Meeting, Prepared by the Executive Committee of the SBC, (Nashville, TN. 2007), p.78.

7 Mark Matlock, "From Wacky to Wise," *Youth Workers Journal*, May/June 2006.

8 David Wheaton, *University of Destruction* , (Minneapolis, Minnesota: Bethany House, 2005), p.14.

9 George Barna, *Real Teens* (Regal Books, 2001), p.136.

10 Glen Schultz, Taken from: KingdomEducation.com.

11 Jeremy and Jerusha Clark, *After You Drop Them Off: A Parent's Guide to Student Ministry*. (Colorado Springs, Waterbrook Press, 2005) p.192.

12 Ron Luce, *Battle Cry for a Generation* (Colorado Springs: Cook Communication Ministries, 2005), pp.21-22.

13 LifeWay Research, 2007, Taken from: http://www.lifeway.com/lwc/article_main_page/0%2C1703%2CA%25253D165950%252526M%25253D200906%2C00.html.

14 *USA Today*, Aug. 6, 2007, Taken from: http://www.usatoday.com/news/religion/2007-08-06-church-drop-outs_N.htm.

15 Alvin Reid, *Raising the Bar: Ministry to Youth in the New Millennium* (Grand Rapids, MI: Kregel Publications, 2004), p.35.

16 Ibid., p.45.

17 Associations of Youth Ministry Educators Survey, 2002.

18 Lillian Kwon, "Study: State of High School Seniors Today," www.christianpost.com, October 24, 2006

19 Leon Tucker, a personal mentor of mine and my supervising pastor, has been an encouragement to me in this area.

20 Jonathan Grenz, "Factors Influencing Job or Career Changes Among Youth ministers," Taken from: http://ayme.gosp##com.net/jym_article.php?article_id=25, Fall 2002.

21 The 7-Year Plan is available at www.pray.org\students.

22 Alvin Reid, *Raising the Bar*, pp.38-39.

23 Thom Rainer, as quoted in bpnews.net/bpnews.asp?ID=20724.

24 Baptism information taken from the North American Mission Board as reported in a Baptist Press article "Baptisms Down Amid Other Growth," Russ Rankin, April 17, 2007. Population information taken from wikipedia.org.

25 Cathy Lynn Grossman, "Rite of Baptism Trickles Away" *USA Today*, April 16, 2006.

26 Greg Stier, *Outbreak: Creating a Contagious Youth Ministry through Viral Evangelism*, (Chicago: Moody Publishers, 2002).

27 Thom Rainer, *Effective Evangelistic Churches* (Broadman & Holman, Nashville, 1996) p.22.

28 Nehemiah Institute, Inc. PEERS Trend Chart and Explanation, Lexington, KY, 2004. Taken from: www.nehemiahinstitute.com.

29 As reported in *Beyond Belief to Convictions* by Josh McDowell, p.9.

30 Jerry Adler, "In Search of the Spiritual," *Newsweek*, September 5, 2005, p.48-49.

31 Josh McDowell, p.15.

32 Christian Smith, *Soul Searching* (New York, NY: Oxford University Press, 2005), p.267.

33 Ibid.

34 Merton Strommen and Richard Hardel, *Passing on the Faith*,(Winona, MI: Saint Mary's Press, 2000), p.198.

35 Sonja Steptoe Bellflower, "In Touch With Jesus," *Time* Magazine, October 31, 2006

revaLUe:

Shifting the
Values of
Student Ministry

Do you recall how you felt when the first church hired you to lead its student ministry? Although I was a young bi-vocational student pastor at the time, I honestly remember believing that if my teens at Northlake Baptist Church were to sell out totally for Christ that we could turn the world upside down. After almost twenty years, I still vividly remember all the students in my first youth group and can say all fourteen names from memory. When I think back to my years at Northlake, I can't help but laugh and think that it is a miracle of God that I have survived this long in ministry. I had no idea about student ministry or what student pastors were supposed to do. Because of this, I planned my entire ministry out of the only book that was in my office—a 1980s Youth Specialties' clipart book. If there was a cool clip art picture, I was sure to put it on our calendar: Rambo water-wars, youth choir, grub camp, mission trips, lock-ins, lock-outs, rock-a-thons, greased pig chases. I was a man with passion but without a clue.

> Most student pastors are like I was, too busy planning a calendar, filling teacher slots, putting out fires, and running a pace that isn't sustainable or healthy to stop and honestly rethink what we value as student pastors.

I remember one Wednesday night getting unbelievably angry at a student named Ricky. After a night of him repeatedly jamming his finger into me, I told him if he touched me one more time I was going to hit him as hard as I could. My threat would make him leave me alone, right? Wrong. Within seconds he had stuck his finger into the side of my neck once again, and I then faced my first student ministry conundrum. Do I hit a student in the mouth or tell a lie? Quickly reasoning that a punch was the lesser of the two sins I hit Ricky as hard as I could, just as I had promised. I admit that it was tough teaching later that night on the series I had recently begun on the beatitudes... "Blessed are the peacemakers."

Fortunately for me our church had an environment of grace, and Ricky's dad forgave me. I didn't understand a lot of things, not the least of which was not to bloody a teen's nose before youth group. The truth of the matter was that when it came to student ministry I didn't know what I was doing, and my values were nowhere close to correct. I valued those parents who would let a twenty-something youth leader take their kids anywhere he wanted rather than those parents who were more discerning. I valued being busy and thought that my full calendar meant I was reaching students. I valued the events that drew a crowd rather than those where the Word was faithfully taught. I only valued my ministry's role in the students' lives and rarely helped students value the role of the church as a whole. I valued the applause of people, being needed, and hearing the phrase "If we didn't have you around here, I don't know what we would do." Where did I get the idea to value those things? I don't think it was intentional; I simply adopted the student ministry value system of those days, and I believe that today's value system isn't all that different.

Perhaps you often step back and look at the big picture of your student ministry. However, most student pastors are like I was, too busy planning a calendar, filling teacher slots, putting out fires, and running a pace that isn't sustainable or healthy to stop and honestly rethink what we value as student pastors. Today's research is showing us that the current value system in student ministry is not generating the returns we hoped it would. I find myself like a person in a store doing a double-take at the price tags wondering how the values got so mixed up. It is time to step back, check the price tags, and do some revaluing of our current system. I'm afraid we may find that in many cases the price is wrong. To help us revalue student ministry, we'll look at four areas in light of today's research and biblical precedent, and you can assign the greater value to whichever item you think deserves it. They are:

- Separation from parents or partnership with parents?

- Student ministry or student development?

- Cultural relevance or biblical faithfulness?

- Internalized ministries or championing the church?

SEPARATION FROM PARENTS OR PARTNERSHIP WITH PARENTS?

Over the past few years, I have been given several opportunities to speak about a biblical framework for student ministry. We all want our ministries to be biblically based, and we all know the importance of parents as primary spiritual disciplers. From talking with many student pastors who shared their struggles about how to put these principles in place, I have heard the following:

- "Student ministry wouldn't be nearly as difficult if it didn't involve dealing with parents."
- "I don't know if our parents are on the same page with me and my ministry."
- "I don't think too many of our parents desire to disciple their children."
- "Our parents see spiritual formation exclusively as my job."
- I even had one student pastor ask, "How do you involve parents if every parent in your ministry is an idiot?"

We live in a society that has become increasingly specialized in providing services. You name it, and you can pay someone to do it for you. Just open up the phone book to find someone to wash your dog, clean your gutters, buy your groceries, tutor your children, or watch your kids. Some parents and churches unfortunately view student ministry in the same way: as a spiritual drop-off service best left to the professionals. Those parents think they are only responsible to take their child to church—put him or her in a spiritual environment and out comes a morally sound young adult. They are then angry when things do not turn out as expected and demand an explanation from a student pastor they barely know or may have never met. What's missing from this scenario?

Before we go to pointing the fingers solely at the parents, churches must also shoulder some of the blame. Student pastors may have too quickly accepted responsibility for teens' spirituality and may be too reluctant to remind and equip parents to take their responsibility as primary spiritual disciplers. I have often seen parents hand the baton of spiritual formation off to me over the years, but it's not mine to take. Traditional student ministry has come to value freedom from parents and neglect the importance of partnership with them. The problem with this value system is twofold: 1) it isn't biblical and 2) it doesn't work. The research is now pointing this fact out to us.

In Bob Altemeyer and Bruce Hunsberger's book *Amazing Conversions*, we are told the stories of forty-six college freshmen they call the "Amazing Apostates." These students were identified in a survey of more than two thousand college freshmen as being among those who were raised in church-going, Christian families but had abandoned their faith by the time they reached college. Here are a few excerpts from their extensive research:

- All of the different approaches to studying parental influences in the religious socialization process converge on a single conclusion: Parents play an extremely important role in developing religious attitudes and practices of their offspring. In fact, few researchers would quarrel with the conclusion that parents are the most important influence in this regard.[1]
- We acquire our religion from our parents almost as certainly as we inherit the color of our eyes.[2]
- You can make a pretty good prediction of whether or

not a university student, raised as a Christian, will still accept Christianity if you know how much the family religion was emphasized while he was growing up.[3]

- Parents of those who "kept the faith" emphasized religion twice as much as the parents of those who became apostates.[4]
- If today's young people seem less religious than their parents, it may be traced to their parents' neglecting to pass on the grandparents' training.[5]
- During their research they asked these freshmen to identify who or what they most turned to when they experienced doubts or questions specifically in regards to religion and their faith. The responses were, in order:
  - Talking with parents
  - Reading the Bible
  - Talking with friends
  - Spending time in prayer
  - Talking to a minister or religious leader
  - Going to a camp or retreat to renew their faith.[6]

Research and common sense tell us the importance of parents in the future success of teens, but it also points to the role of the church. What is needed, and is rarely the case, is a partnership between church and parents. However, the current student ministry model has come to value freedom from parents because it seems more convenient to minister to students without parents overseeing the process. Parents are often seen as a hindrance to ministry, as a source of endless opinions and criticism, and in extreme cases as a necessary evil. Ironically, in many churches parents don't feel welcome in the very ministry supposedly partnering with them to instill a biblical worldview in their children. We must identify strategic ways to create a partnership that goes beyond a drop-off service with monthly parent newsletters and an annual parents' meeting. In the current student ministry model:

- Parents have little or no input as primary disciplers into what is shaping their child's life. There is little carryover or continuation of what happens at home and at church.
- Spiritual formation becomes viewed as only something that happens at church by the students and their parents. The obvious problem is that most teens are only at church a few hours a week compared to the dozens of hours they spend at home.
- Our ministries fail to be sharpened and enhanced by those with whom we say we have locked arms.
- Because parents aren't engaged it seems the only time parents come to staff is when something has gone wrong or if they have a complaint.
- A major reason student pastors don't last long in most churches is because many of them fail to realize the importance of having a support team of parents that prays for, encourages, advises, and serves as advocates for them.
- The role of the parents is diminished, minimizing or

eliminating any partnership between church and family, which causes both to suffer.

Johnny Derouen, PhD, student ministry professor at Southwestern Seminary said:

For many years we have thought of a parent ministry as consisting of a parent newsletter/e-mails, a first-of-the-year luncheon to discuss the upcoming year, and a monthly parent meeting where we cover a parent topic. Yet none of these are headed anywhere—they are just shotgun blasts. Parent ministry needs to be thought through as thoroughly as student ministry. Where do we want our parents to be at the end of this year and when their child turns 18? What will it take to get them there and to equip them to do their job as parents? Where do I want my parents to be in 3 or 6 years? Most of us have no idea, therefore our meetings are good but do not build or aim the parents in any direction.[7]

Student ministry from a biblical framework views parents as indispensable ministry partners. Imagine for a moment what it could look like if parents and the church were working off the same sheet to develop the next generation. Imagine what it could look like if student pastors spent time with parents creating a clear plan of action where both church and family knew what they needed to do to help grow godly adults. For those students whose parents don't participate, imagine the impact if they were introduced to loving family environments that modeled and educated them as to what a Christian marriage and family should look like. Consider what it would mean to parents if they were taught to prioritize a lasting legacy that affected generations. We must begin to champion the God-given role of parents and revalue our student ministry so that student pastors, volunteers, and parents see each other as essential partners in ministry.

STUDENT MINISTRY OR STUDENT DEVELOPMENT?

One of my fellow pastors and I were talking at a retreat about his years in student ministry. It's not hard to see his gifts and his love for the Lord, so I was shocked to hear about the time he almost walked away from ministry. He had decided he was going to open a Christmas tree farm, and he had already picked out the land and begun making plans. He was going to escape from it all. Why would a guy with such gifts give up on ministry? He pointed to the value system that said, "Bigger is always better"; if there were 600 students at one of his student ministry events, then he would need 700 at the next one; if he somehow through God's providence baptized 100 students this year, then he better begin praying now for 150 next year. He experienced firsthand the pressure to keep the current model of student ministry going. He realized what it was doing to his walk with the Lord and his family, and he decided to walk away. It's not that he wasn't cut out for ministry; the opposite is the case: he simply couldn't survive in the current student ministry value system and was brave enough to admit that.

I hear more and more student pastors frustrated by the aspects of their student ministries that aren't ministry. Guys are busier than ever trying to keep the student ministry machine going, while they are losing those they were intended to care for. It's as if they spend all their time running from event to event and activity to activity knowing that the busyness is preventing them from focusing on what will last. Student ministry in many cases has become the local YMCA or teen amusement park; students check in and out, but mostly out. After all, once they have experienced years of fun-and-games, all-you-can-eat, no-responsibility, free-from-parents amusement, then we have helped train their appetites for pleasure to find more alluring fulfillment in the adult world.

Students were asked what they wanted to see more of in student ministry in a study of high school seniors by Fuller Seminary's Center for Youth and Family Ministry (CYFM). The top answer was a desire for more service projects. Number two was deep conversations, followed by mission trips, accountability, and more time in worship. A desire for more games came in last.[8] The Barna Group found a similar result when the most common reason students gave for attending church was "to better understand what I believe."[9]

Think about the biblical precedent for ministry. Paul's desire for Timothy wasn't about fun and games; he wanted to develop him to be grounded and able to defend his faith. Jesus spent most of His time developing His twelve disciples, knowing that He had entrusted great truth to them. Have we made it our goal to just keep our young people busy and by doing so think that we have kept them out of trouble? A student pastor told me that his pastor's perspective was: "People are going to be busy with something, so we might as well keep them busy at the church." In our efforts to spiritually quarantine students, we aren't preparing them for a world that is asking tough life questions for which they must have answers. In order to prepare them for life after graduation, we have to spend more time developing students and those who greatly influence them and less time on the machine that demands more and more.

A glimpse into the typical student ministry value system is captured by Mark Yaconelli. He says:

Other youth ministries are created in response to adolescent anxieties. Noticing young people's discomfort with adult forms of faith and desperately seeking to keep youth engaged, some churches develop ministries of distraction. Inspired by parachurch youth ministries from the 1950s, like Youth for Christ and Young Life (whose founder, Jim Rayburn, once wrote a book entitled *It's a Sin to Bore a Kid*), ministries of distraction keep youth moving from one activity to the next: rafting trips, pizza parties, game nights, ski retreats, beach fests, music festivals, amusement parks, taco-feeds, scavenger-hunts, 45 crowd-breakers, raves, skits, and whatever other activities attract kids. It's a Nickelodeon approach to youth ministry that seeks to appeal to kids' propensity for fun and recreation. This is how churches respond to youth who cry "Church is boring!" It's the ministry of excitement; discipleship through fun, culture-friendly, "Christian-lite" events. Like parents who pop in a video to entertain the kids when relatives arrive, the idea is to keep the young people from running out, to keep them in the general vicinity of the church, to keep them happy until they're mature enough to join the congregation...

While such ministries may keep youth entertained, they often keep youth distracted from the deeper rhythms and practices of the Christian faith. Programs and activities are chosen based on the level of excitement that's generated. No one wants to act like an adult for fear of scaring the kids. Leaders become hesitant to engage youth in any activity that is in contrast to the consumer culture. Prayer, spiritual exercises, theological conversation, and spiritual disciplines that challenge the status quo are dumped out of fear that youth may cry "This is like school!" or "You're just like our parents!" or (worst of all) "This is boring." So the ministry never addresses the deeper needs of youth, never challenges them to explore the alternative way of Jesus. Like children's television programming that seeks to keep kids attentive so they'll watch the commercials, our ministries of diversion respond to young people's most carnal appetites so we can slip in a five-minute Bible study or parade them through the church building.[10]

Do you ever feel that "student ministry" has taken a life of its own or that you spend more time focused on event-driven student ministry? As soon as one event is over, it seems that three more wait, while all the time bystanders are willing to suggest four or five more activities the church down the street is doing. The events are planned and crowds may come, but how can we be sure we really reached them? How can we be sure they have been developed? What do you think would happen in the typical student ministry if the leadership announced, "We are canceling all student ministry events and activities. We want to take this next year to focus on our students becoming true disciples, therefore our student ministry calendar will look completely different next year"?

As we saw in the first chapter, the student ministry machine also plows over student pastors and their families.

Doug Fields knows the struggle all too well. He writes about his first ten years in ministry, saying:

> Because in the busyness of my first decade of
> ministry, I abandoned my first love (God) and
> developed a love affair with *doing* ministry. I turned
> into the poster child for doing at the expense of being.
> I was always busy, always on the move, always
> armed with new ideas and fresh visions that had to
> be implemented and conquered immediately... but
> at the expense of *being* a man after God's own heart.
> I was too busy for God—but I figured God would
> understand because I was busy *for* him... I just sacri-
> ficed my intimacy with God for the idols of busyness,
> achievement and making people happy. While others
> were applauding my "success," I was an empty shell
> in spiritual atrophy.[11]

I am not suggesting that all student ministries are too busy to develop teens. Maybe your group is full of developed teenagers, grounded in the Word and able to articulate their beliefs. But how do you know? Here's a way to see. At your next meeting, pass out blank sheets of paper with one question across the top: "Why do you believe that Jesus is the Messiah?" Explain to your group that they will have fifteen minutes to answer the question; the only rule is that if they use a Bible verse, they must cite its source. If they mention a prophecy, tell them to be specific on which one they are referencing. Then turn them loose. Give it a try. You may be amazed at the results.

But why this question? You might recall that this is essentially the same question that Jesus asked His disciples in Matthew 16:15—"Who do you say I am?" It is also the same one that John the Baptist pondered as he sat in a jail cell before he was beheaded and sent his followers to ask, "Is Jesus really the one?" (Luke 7:19). It is also the same question our teens will ask when the trials of life come—and they will come—as world religions, university professors, atheists, and moments of doubt challenge our students. Has today's model prepared our students to answer this basic and foundational question?

> My fear is likely the same as yours: Will that teen who is consistently at our student ministry events be able to clearly articulate one of the most important and foundational truths?

I'll be honest; a reality check like that scares me a little. My fear is likely the same as yours: will that teen who is consistently at our student ministry events be able to clearly articulate one of the most important and foundational truths? Sadly, student pastors who evaluate their progress like this will see that many of the students who come week after week, year after year are not being developed. Many of our "core" kids aren't core kids at all; they are fringe kids who come for carnival games and cotton-candy messages. We must have the guts to admit that many of the hours our students spend at our events aren't truly equipping them; many of our events are more dessert and less meat. It is time to value student development over traditional, event-driven student ministry.

CULTURAL RELEVANCE OR BIBLICAL FAITHFULNESS?

What will youth ministry and the church look like in ten years? This is a great question that Dr. Richard Ross, professor of student ministry at Southwestern Seminary, recently explored. He predicts:

Across the next ten years, some churches will get better and better at doing the wrong thing – with excellence. For a while, they will appear to be successful. Such churches will build buildings to support segregation – and they will do so with excellence. These churches will use focus-group research in order to design Starbucks-on-steroids buildings for adults. In the 1980s, adults paid age-group ministers to do their work for them. In the 1990s, they added paid interns to further guarantee that they would not be called on for help. Ten years from now, perhaps the entire age-group staff will be paid by those who enjoy escaping into a pleasant world of adults. Providing services to church members will be the clear priority.[12]

Bigger is better in today's prevailing church-growth philosophy. Many times the invitation to meet Christ at the foot of the cross seems much less appealing than the new tricks of the trade that some churches are embracing in the effort to be culturally relevant. Student ministries today look to gimmicks, giveaways, hype, and featured artists as ploys to attract teens rather than calling people to biblical repentance and obedience.

Doug Fields writes:

> What I had idealized as a stroll in the park became a race on the freeway. This ministry culture—filled with overwhelming pressures to perform and please, as well as plenty of resulting heartache—would eventually take its toll on my joy, my spiritual health, and ultimately my ministry effectiveness... The church decision-makers made it clear to me that *bigger* was always *better*. Masses were desired over health. *More* was the main value, goal, and gauge for success.[13]

Today's evangelism is striving after new and innovative ways to make the gospel seem more palatable to unbelievers. John MacArthur correctly identifies the problem by saying, "Churches invest endless effort, creativity, and dollars in new ways of packaging an age-old message, so that it will seem more useful to unchurched Harry and Mary."[14]

He continues:

Today churches often use gimmicks and entertainment to try to get people into the church. That is a sign that people aren't following a biblical pattern. It quite often functions like a business rather than a body, a factory rather than a family, and a corporation rather than a community.[15]

Churches oftentimes put their effort towards making Christ culturally relevant, (which in itself is an oxymoron) in an effort to get or win more people. Check your church mail; the countless flyers you receive for conferences that are highlighted by cultural trends, innovative secular suggestions, and MTV/pop-culture solutions to build more attractive ministries will show you proof of what student ministry values. They tell you that relevance is the key to growing a successful ministry and reaching students. Don't misunderstand; relevance is needed, and we want to be relevant to this generation, but have we placed a greater value on being culturally trendy than on faithfully presenting the Word?

Let's face it; the gospel becomes a tougher sale when many of our churches seek to offer a buffet of "spiritual" options with an unbridled consumer desire. David Wells reminds us:

Can churches really hide their identity without losing their religious character? Can the Church view people as consumers without inevitably forgetting that they are sinners? Can the Church promote the Gospel as a product and not forget that those who buy it must repent? Can the Church market itself and not forget that it does not belong to itself but to Christ? Can the Church pursue success in the marketplace and not lose its biblical faithfulness?[16]

Wells warns that when our purpose for existence begins with "get more people" rather than "glorifying God," we soon begin to entertain every imaginable possibility, biblical or not, to attract people.[17] Our churches' values are exposed when the first questions after every ministry event are: "How many came?" rather than "Did this event give a glimpse of the glory of God?" "How many responded?" rather than "Were families and the church championed?" "How many came forward for baptism?" rather than "How will we disciple those who responded to become faithful followers of Christ, mature in their faith?" It is time to trust Jesus' words in John 12:32: "But I, when I am lifted up from the earth, I will draw all men to myself." Instead, we often think that He needs to

> Our goal as student pastors isn't to simply help students get through the pitfalls of high school, although that is part of the assignment. Our biblical commission is to build disciples of Christ.

be repackaged or changed to be relevant to our teens.

My goal is not to be an alarmist or pessimist; it is to face the brutal facts and ask the tough questions: Are we cheapening the Scripture's call with a win-a-prize mentality of the gospel? Do we spend more time on video editing and game planning than we do preparing and praying over biblical messages? Are we equipping students with the tools they need to deal with life's challenges and questions when God's Word is always squeezed behind a program filled with pizza, prizes, and gimmicks? What are we teaching teens to value when our event is built around MTV or the latest reality show? Could Dietrich Bonhoeffer's statement below apply to today's student ministry?

> Cheap grace is the deadly enemy of our Church. We are fighting today for costly grace. Cheap grace means grace sold on the market like cheapjacks' wares. The sacraments, the forgiveness of sin, and the consolations of religion are thrown away at cut prices...cheap grace is the preaching of forgiveness without requiring repentance, baptism without church discipline, communion without confession, absolution without personal confession. Cheap grace is grace without discipleship, grace without the cross, grace without Jesus Christ, living and incarnate.[18]

Our goal as student pastors isn't to simply help students get through the pitfalls of high school, although that is part of the assignment. Our biblical commission is to build disciples of Christ—"Therefore go and make disciples of all nations, baptizing them in the name of the Father and of the Son and of the Holy Spirit, and teaching them to obey everything I have commanded you" (Matthew 28:19-20). We as leaders must provide clear biblical direction and honestly evaluate our own path in light of a church culture that many times prioritizes business models over biblical principles. The basic truth of the gospel is that we are inviting men and women to the cross. Mark 8:34 says, "If anyone would come after me, he must deny himself and take up his cross and follow me." The weight of that verse will create more true disciples than any publicity stunt can.

Did Paul ask young Timothy to entertain the crowds and plan massive events with the new converts until the New Testament was finished? No, he exhorted him, "Until I come, devote yourself to the public reading of Scripture, to preaching and to teaching" (1 Timothy 4:13). Current trends will not sustain our students when the trials of life hit them, and they will come. An MTV-packaged ministry will not encourage students to serve the church when the real show isn't really about them. A theology-lite message will not prepare students who will live in an information-driven society that will demand real answers. Only faithfully teaching the Bible can do that. "All Scripture is God-breathed and is useful for teaching, rebuking, correcting and training in righteousness, so that the man of God may be thoroughly equipped for every good work" (2 Timothy 3:16-17).

Today's model of student ministry tells us that relevancy

is critical, and many of us who talk about the sufficiency of the Bible are perceived as old-school. Erwin Luzter says it like this:

> When the Bible, which is rooted in the soil of history and logic, is either rejected or reinterpreted to fit any belief, everyone is on his own to guess at the answer for ultimate questions... As a result, the Christian church is floundering, looking for an answer to today's spiritual and moral malaise. When we tell people we must return to the Bible, we often are pitied, looked upon as sincere but naïve souls whom time has passed by.[19]

The Bible doesn't need clever repackaging to change lives. Jesus doesn't need an image consultant or PR firm to make an impact on today's generation of teens. Our student ministry events don't have to be themed around the latest trend to reach students. While we must value creativity and relevance to teens, we must put the greater value on being sure that the Bible is faithfully taught in our ministries.

INTERNALIZED MINISTRIES OR CHAMPIONING THE CHURCH?

There is a new term, "graduating from God," that is used to describe our student retention rate. I really don't like to hear this term even though research reveals its accuracy. My mind thinks immediately of the ornate, beautiful, large churches across Europe that sit nearly empty each week. Obviously, things were going quite well at one point as congregations built these massive edifices. I wonder what went wrong, and I wonder how we can ensure our bigger-and-better church buildings never one day sit empty.

I am troubled when I hear student pastors today speak exclusively of their ministries without much mention of the church as a whole. It appears that as our ministries become more internalized and specialized, there is more temptation for turfism and a siloed-ministry approach. It is easy to run your race with very little contact with other ministries in the church. Staff members battle to outperform one another in a spiritual game of one-upmanship instead of locking arms, "esteeming others better than ourselves" and serving others for the common good. As our pastoral teams operate in this value system, they view the needs of a few people as more important than the priority and mission of the church as a whole. Staff members increasingly see this separation as normal in many church contexts. Our students then catch

> It appears that as our ministries become more internalized and specialized, there is more temptation for turfism and a siloed-ministry approach. It is easy to run your race with very little contact with other ministries in the church.

the same values and fall in love with student ministry instead of falling in love with the church. Students then graduate from student events and student worship and student small groups, and therefore graduate from the church and graduate from God as they graduate from school.

David Kinnaman, author of *Ministry to Mosaics*, says:

Let us examine one of the most uncomfortable realities of youth ministry. In the typical church, 3 out of every 5 teens will be unchurched in the next 10 to 12 years. At your next youth meeting look around. Chances are most of those teenagers will disengage from church attendance by age 30. In fact, participation in church steadily declines following high school graduation, bottoming out during a person's late 20s. Sadly, many of these people will describe their teenage involvement in church as a "Jesus phase."[20]

When we have students leaving the church at the rate we are losing them we must address several issues:

- We must educate our students concerning the important purpose of the church as a whole.
- We must champion the church before our students with a biblical passion.
- We must provide for our students opportunities to serve the church and its mission.
- We must help our students see the church impacting the

community and the world in which they live.

• We must demonstrate an authentic, faithful, unselfish leadership before our students that is winsome for the church.

A biblical framework of student ministry must value serving, supporting, and championing the church. We must teach teens to value the church as a whole, and not just the student ministry. Ephesians 5 tells us about the value Christ places on the church. It tells us that Christ is the head of the church (v. 23), that He gave Himself up for the church (v. 25), that He nourishes and cherishes the church (v. 29), and that He loves the church (v. 25). David Jeremiah explains Christ's love for the church by saying:

> The Greek word *agape* is one of the most important words in the New Testament. It means unconditional Love–the no-strings-attached love with which God loves us. *Agape*'s Hebrew parallel in the Old Testament, *hesed*, is less familiar but no less important. It means loyal love and describes God's everlasting love for His people, Israel and Israel's spiritual descendants, the church.[21]

Are we building that kind of love for the church in our students? Are we modeling that kind of love for the church in how we do ministry? When students are separated from the life of the church for most of its services, activities, and ministries, we are setting them up for failure. Those who graduate from God after high school are proof that the transition back into the "real church world" is much harder for them than we think. I am not saying we should eliminate all age-graded ministry and keep the children and students in adult church events. We age-grade our Sunday morning and discipleship groups because we understand the value of the time spent growing with others in a similar stage of life. However, we must decide if our current ministry values are inadvertently beginning the process that turns them away or if our student ministry is championing the role of the church in their lives.

> **We must decide if our current ministry values are inadvertently beginning the process that turns them away or if our student ministry is championing the role of the church in their lives.**

REVALUE

One of the goals of our student ministry is to take our students on a foreign mission trip before they graduate from high school. We typically begin our Belize mission experience by visiting our friends at King's Orphanage. It's a very encouraging and challenging time to see the living conditions of fifty-five to sixty children in a 3,000-square-foot house and to attend their evening worship service. The children pack into a very small room, and the older children serve as worship leaders. I have never heard praise and singing that is more heartfelt. One can see it in how the children are truly grateful for all the blessings, few as they may be in our students' eyes, God has given to them. They then begin to quote scriptures, not by the verse but by the chapter, and many times entire books of the Bible. The second day we typically attend church services in Dangregra and Light of the Valley. Our students always comment on the hard pews, the lack of air conditioning, the outhouses, the buzzing in the broken sound system, and the lack of space. They, however, also see the passionate singing and the genuine expression of worship. Somewhere in all of this, our students begin to realize what it means to be thankful, to worship, and to serve. They begin to realize that they are surrounded by students their own age who are much more mature in their faith, and our students quickly realize they learn much more from these students from a third-world country than they can teach. In short, they are being ministered to instead of doing the ministry. I always wonder how these churches with no big events, no budget, and no full-time pastors can produce

> It may be a hard pill to swallow, but the price is wrong; our value system is skewed. We must reclaim a biblical value system for student ministry before it is too late.

such fully committed followers of Christ. I am left with the thought that they must have assigned value very differently than our American churches have.

I have never met a student pastor who works the hours he does who is willing to accept the results that research today is revealing, but many don't know how to address the problem. Students are graduating from God, or in many cases leave even earlier, when they get their driver's licenses. It is sad to admit that for many students as soon as there is an option other than church, they take it. It may be a hard pill to swallow, but the price is wrong; our value system is skewed. We must reclaim a biblical value system for student ministry before it is too late. We need to partner with parents, develop students, remain faithful to the Word, and champion the church in the lives of our young people. In short, we must reclaim a biblical value system and reexamine the framework the Bible gives for ministering to students.

NOTES

1 Bob Altemeyer and Bruce Hunsberger, *Amazing Conversions* (Prometheus Books, 1997) p.226.

2 Ibid. p.10.

3 Ibid. p.11.

4 Ibid. p.11.

5 Ibid. p.11.

6 Ibid. p.18.

7 E-mail received from Dr. Derouen on February 7, 2007.

8 Lillian Kwon, "Study: State of High School Seniors Today," posted on www.christianpost.com, October 24, 2006.

9 Ibid.

10 Mark Yaconelli, *Contemplative Youth Ministry* (Zondervan/Youth Specialties, 2006) taken from youthspecialties.com/store/samples/pdf/c/cymch.pdf.

11 Doug Fields, *What Matters Most- When NO Is Better than YES* (Zondervan/Youth Specialties, 2006) pp.11-12.

12 Richard Ross, "Youth Ministry and the Church in Ten years," *National Network of Youth Workers Magazine*, 2006, vol.24, no.4, p.7.

13 Doug Fields, *What Matters Most*, pp.26-27.

14 John MacArthur, *The Master Plan for the Church* (Chicago: Moody Publishers, 1991) p.83.

15 Ibid.

16 David Wells, *Losing Our Virtue* (Grand Rapids: Eerdmans Publishing, 1998) p.202.

17 David Wells, *Above All Earthly Powers* (Grand Rapids: Eerdmans Publishing, 2005) p.263.

18 Dietrich Bonhoeffer, *The Cost of Discipleship,* Revised and Unabridged Edition, (New York: The MacMillan Company, 1967) pp.45-47.

19 Erwin W. Lutzer, *Seven Reasons Why You Can Trust the Bible* (Chicago: Moody Press, 1998) pp.11-12.

20 Information gathered from http://enrichmentjournal.ag.org/200604/200604_028_MosaicGen.cfm.

21 David Jeremiah, *Turning Points* (Integrity Publishing, Brentwood, TN, 2005) p.40.

reMODeL:

A Biblical

Framework for

Student Ministry

"Can you articulate a biblical framework for student ministry?" I began wrestling with the question almost a decade ago when a close friend asked me this in a meeting.[1] I went through the standard lines about how the Bible doesn't address the topic directly and gave a few biblical principles of which most in our profession are aware, but the question would not stop gnawing at me. Is it the parents' or the church's job to disciple teens? How can the church partner with parents? Was the ministry that I have built over the past years truly biblical?

From that point I have approached the Bible with an open mind to identify its framework for student ministry, even if that means adopting a model that is different than what we have inherited. What I have found is both ancient and cutting edge, simple to understand and complex to implement. So where do we start? A biblical model must be based on that which the Bible emphasizes rather than starting with the gimmicks hyped at the most recent conference.

There in the first book of the Old Testament, God began the first and primary institution for discipleship: the family. Then in the first book of the New Testament, we see a second institution established, also with a job of discipling: the church. If these are the two institutions championed in the Word, then we must do the same. Instead, today we find Christian families disintegrating and more students fleeing the church than ever before. Something has got to change. To have a biblical framework for student ministry, we must shift our ministry framework to match the emphases the Bible places on the family and the church.

> If these are the two institutions championed in the Word, then we must do the same. Instead, today we find Christian families disintegrating and more students fleeing the church than ever before.

In short, our ministries must co-champion the family and the church. Co-champion? Even the term is a little uncomfortable for us. We want one champion, one Super Bowl winner, one collegiate national champion, one world champion boxer rather than half a dozen. The idea of co-champions, even in discipling teenagers, is too fuzzy and not flashy enough to sell out a student ministry conference. For too long what has been missing is a co-championing mentality that places equal importance on family and church. Parents have, in most church contexts, handed over their biblically assigned task as primary disciplers to a church pastor who has been taught to accept it. Some people, in other contexts, have made a case to abolish student ministry, remove teens from student activities, and try to disciple their kids while excluding the church. Neither is biblical. Neither is ideal. The two institutions must step closer to one another to be based on a biblical model. Teens need family and church working hand-in-hand surrounding them with truth and godly models to follow. To find the biblical model for student ministry, let's look at what the Bible says about each institution.

CHAMPIONING THE FAMILY

When I am asked to speak at conferences on how to implement a more strategic biblical framework for ministry, I always start by asking the same question: "As you read through God's Word, who do you find God gave the *primary role* of a child's spiritual formation?" In other words, "To whom did God assign this important job?" The response is always the same. Hands go up in the room, and without fail the correct answer is always given: "Parents!" Then comes the tougher question: "Are you open to considering whether we believe this fact more in theory than we do in practice?"

God developed the idea of family. Sure, that sounds like a simplistic fact shared in an elementary Sunday School class, but its implications are anything but simple. In Genesis 1:27-28 we read, "God created man in his own image, in the image of God he created him; male and female he created them. God blessed them and said to them, 'Be fruitful and increase in number.'" Genesis 2:24 says, "For this reason, a man will leave his father and mother and be united to his wife, and they will become one flesh." God started the first family and ordained it as the institution for not only reproduction but also primary discipleship. Think of Deuteronomy 6:4-9:

> Hear, O Israel: The LORD our God, the LORD is one. Love the LORD your God with all your heart and with all your soul and with all your strength. These commandments that I give you today are to be upon your hearts. Impress them on your children. Talk about them when you sit at home and when you walk along the road, when you lie down and when you get up. Tie them as symbols on your hands and bind them on your foreheads. Write them on the doorframes of your houses and on your gates.

The importance of this passage, called the Shema, is magnified when we consider the practice of Orthodox Jews who recite it twice a day, morning and evening. Of all the great Old Testament passages concerning creation, faith, God's provisions, the coming Messiah, commandments, repentance, and forgiveness, I am amazed that it was this passage that God impressed on them to repeat daily. We also know that in case we missed the importance the first time, the Lord repeated these same instructions to parents in Deuteronomy 11. All this repetition is more than coincidence; it makes it clear that the Shema is one of the most important passages in the Old Testament, as it instructs parents with their God-given assignment to disciple their children. If it is a foundational principle in the Bible, then it should also be one of the most important foundations of our student ministries. God places the primary responsibility on parents, and how we do ministry must reflect that fact. Tedd Tripp comments on the Shema saying,

> Deuteronomy 6 underscores this view of parental responsibility. In verse 3, God says His goal is for the Israelites and their children and grandchildren to fear the Lord by keeping His decrees. The person by whom God's decrees are passed on is the parent whom God calls to train His children when they sit at home, when they walk by the road, when they lie down, and when they rise up. God has an objective. He wants one generation to follow another in His ways. God accomplishes this objective through the agency of parental instruction.[2]

Other scriptures that instruct parents on how to disciple their children are:

- Psalm 78:1-7: O my people, hear my teaching; listen to the words of my mouth. I will open my mouth in parables, I will utter hidden things, things from of old—what we have heard and known, *what our fathers have told us.* We will not hide them from their children; *we will tell the next generation* the praiseworthy deeds of the LORD, his power, and the wonders he has done. He decreed statutes for Jacob and established the law in Israel, which *he commanded our forefathers to teach their children, so the next generation* would know them, even the children yet to be born, and they in turn *would tell their children.* Then they would put their trust in God and would not forget his deeds but would keep his commands.

- Ephesians 6:4: *Fathers*, do not exasperate your children; instead, *bring them up* in the training and instruction of the Lord.

- Proverbs 1:8-9: Listen, my son, to your father's instruction and do not forsake your mother's teaching. They will be a garland to grace your head and a chain to adorn your neck.

- Malachi 4:6: He will turn the hearts of the *fathers* to their children, and the hearts of the *children* to their fathers; or else I will come and strike the land with a curse.

- Luke 1:17: And he will go on before the Lord, in the spirit and power of Elijah, to turn the hearts of the *fathers* to their children and the disobedient to the wisdom of the righteous—to make ready a people prepared for the Lord.

- Proverbs 22:6: *Train a child* in the way he should go, and when he is old he will not turn from it.
- Psalm 127:1-4: Unless the LORD builds the house, its builders labor in vain. Unless the LORD watches over the city, the watchmen stand guard in vain. In vain you rise early and stay up late, toiling for food to eat— for he grants sleep to those he loves. *Sons are a heritage from the LORD, children a reward from him.* Like arrows in the hands of a warrior are sons born in one's youth.
- Proverbs 4:1-11: Listen, my sons, to a *father's instruction*; pay attention and gain understanding. I give you sound learning, so do not forsake my teaching. When I was a boy in my father's house, still tender, and an only child of my mother, *he taught me* and said, "Lay hold of my words with all your heart; keep my commands and you will live. Get wisdom, get understanding; do not forget my words or swerve from them. Do not forsake wisdom, and she will protect you; love her, and she will watch over you. Wisdom is supreme; therefore get wisdom. Though it cost all you have, get understanding. Esteem her, and she will exalt you; embrace her, and she will honor you. She will set a garland of grace on your head and present you with a crown of splendor. *Listen, my son*, accept what I say, and the years of your life will be many. I guide you in the way

of wisdom and lead you along straight paths."

- Colossians 3:20-21: *Children*, obey your parents in everything, for this pleases the Lord. *Fathers*, do not embitter your children, or they will become discouraged.

- 1 Thessalonians 2:11-12: For you know that we dealt with each of you *as a father deals with his own children*, encouraging, comforting and urging you to live lives worthy of God, who calls you into his kingdom and glory.

All of us in church leadership are familiar with the qualifications for leadership found in 1 Timothy 3. Here we see the importance of the family yet again stating the leader "*must* manage his own family well and see that his children obey him with proper respect. If anyone does not know how to manage his own family, how can he take care of God's church?" (vv. 4-5). In other words, "Choose men who are respected for the way they are spiritually leading their families." Have you ever wondered why spiritual leadership of family was made a litmus test for church leadership? This verse could have read, "Choose men with a business sense," or "Choose men who pray well," or "Choose men who are givers," or "Choose men who attend worship often." But it doesn't. Why? Nobody knows us like our families do. I believe the Lord wants the church to be led by spiritual leaders, and there is a direct correlation to how a leader is respected at home by those who know him best and his ability to be respected by others. The biblical message is consistent: families are primary.

George Barna summarizes a biblical understanding of parenting well, saying:

> The responsibility for raising spiritual champions, according to the Bible, belongs to the parents. The spiritual nurture of children is supposed to take place in the home. Organizations and people from outside the home might support those efforts, but the responsibility is squarely laid at the feet of the family. This is not a job for specialists. It is a job for parents.[3]

PARENTS ARE PRIMARY

Let's have some fun. See if you can guess where the following quotes are from:

> Studies have shown that parents *are the primary influence* on their children's choices and decisions... and that is why we're proud to offer help to parents. Recognizing that parents have the greatest influence on their children's decisions, the Family Talk program helps... by encouraging open, honest communication between parents and children.[4]

Sounds simple, right? Here's another:

> Nearly three out of four parents believe their children's

friends and classmates have the most influence... Yet contrary to what parents think, kids say mom and dad have the biggest impact on the choices they make.[5]

Maybe a little tougher? Let's do one more:

So you're between the ages of 13 and 24. What makes you happy? A worried, weary parent might imagine the answer to sound something like this: Sex, drugs, a little rock 'n' roll. Maybe some cash, or at least the car keys. Turns out the real answer is quite different. Spending time with family was the top answer to that open-ended question... Parents are seen as an overwhelmingly positive influence in the lives of most young people. Remarkably, nearly half of teens mention at least one of their parents as a hero.[6]

Give up? Maybe multiple choices will help:

a) Focus on the Family
b) Coors Brewing Company
c) American Family Research Council
d) MTV
e) National Network of Youth Ministers
f) Anheuser-Busch Beers

The first quote is from an Anheuser-Busch publication on one of their websites called familytalkonline.com. The second is from MVParents.com, a website of the Coors Brewing Company. The third is from a study conducted by MTV and the Associated Press. Whether it's a Christian organization or a very worldly one, all the research points to the fact that parents are the primary influence of their children. Parents are primary.

An extensive study of 272,400 teenagers conducted by *USA Today Weekend Magazine* found that 70 percent of teens identified their parents as the most important influence in their lives. Twenty-one percent said that about their friends (peers), and only 8 percent named the media (TV shows).[7] This study obviously contradicts cultural misconceptions that peers and media are the primary driving forces for teens. Today's research supports what the Bible has said for thousands of years: parents have the most important place in their child's development.

Christian Smith concluded, in his book *Soul Searching*, after the largest, most in-depth research ever conducted on the spirituality of American teens, that,

> The best way to get most youth more involved in and serious about their faith communities is to get their parents more involved in and serious about their faith communities. For decades in many religious traditions, the prevailing model of youth ministry has relied on pulling teens away from their parents. In some cases, youth ministers have come to see parents as adversaries. There is no doubt a time and place for unique teen

> settings and activities; still, our findings suggest that
> overall youth ministry would probably best be pursued
> in larger context of family ministry, that parents should
> be viewed as indispensable partners in the religious
> formation of youth.[8]

I often wonder if perhaps we have moved so far away from the biblical ideal that we may not recognize it any longer. One very practical way of evaluating how our student ministry is supporting the institution of the family is by reviewing our ministry calendars. Words like "parents," "moms," "dads," and "families" should appear with great regularity on our calendars if our ministries are resourcing, training, and involving parents. Our calendars reveal the reality of what we believe is worth prioritizing. It's a sad reality that in many student ministry contexts if parents were to attend an event, there would be an uneasiness or maybe even a revolt. Mark DeVries, vice president of Youth Builders, reminds us,

> Effective youth ministry in the 21st century is about
> bringing parents back into the picture. No longer can
> the church act as the main dispenser of spiritual forma-
> tion. We need to see ourselves as resources for parents
> in their roles as spiritual formation builders. It's not the
> job of the church to be the only force behind students'
> spiritual formation. It is, and always has been, the role
> of parents.[9]

Richard Ross, spokesperson for the teenage abstinence ministry True Love Waits, said he believes churches should go so far as to build schedules of activities that allow families to have time to "be families." "Churches need to teach parents how to parent, and the Church must teach parents how to spiritually teach and lead every age group of children in their home," he said. "Some churches spend tens of thousands of dollars each year preparing to teach the Bible well at church through curriculums, teacher training and technology, but these same churches are spending zero dollars training parents how to teach the Bible at home.[10] Education coordinators in six major denominations were asked in a study conducted by Effective Christian Education if their congregations were providing classes for parents on effective parenting or communications. Only 8 percent indicated that their congregation was providing such assistance.[11] Ross Campbell correctly says:

> While organized religious instruction and activities
> in churches, Christian camps, and special youth clubs
> are extremely important to your developing child,
> nothing influences him more than his training at home.
> Parents cannot afford to leave spiritual training to other
> people.[12]

Also, churches cannot afford to abdicate the training of parents to TV shows, secular books on the shelves of bookstores, or advice from families in no better shape than they are. The church must train parents how to train.

God assigns the primary responsibility for disciple-ship to parents, therefore our ministries should reflect that principle. Most do not. God's Word champions the family, therefore our ministries must do the same. We do that in two ways. First, we must accept the God-given role of parents as the primary discipler and position our ministry in a family-equipping role. That does not mean we are out of a job; the opposite is true. Our job is bigger than ever, which brings us to the second way we must champion the family—we must equip parents with the tools and understanding to disciple their teens. We will cover this topic in depth in a later chapter, but equipping parents means providing training and events that build a lasting, strong relationship between parents and students. In short, we must work together, championing the family to impact students for a lifetime. Josh McDowell says it best:

> Parents... carry more weight—for good or bad—
> than they give themselves credit for. How a child
> thinks and acts is still molded by his or her home
> life, which means the crumbling foundations of the
> faith among this generation is as much a parental
> problem as a church problem, if not more so. If
> we're going to reclaim the next generation, then the
> home and the church must join forces together like
> never before.[13]

CHAMPIONING THE CHURCH

If the Bible is clear that parents have the primary responsibility to train their children, then shouldn't we shut down all student ministries? Is our calling, our profession, unbiblical? Is student ministry doing more harm than good? I think the answer to all of these questions is no, but you may have been exposed to those who teach otherwise. It seems that there are two polarized views, one focusing on church only while ignoring the family and the other with an exclusive focus on the family. The latter movement is becoming popular in some circles, teaching to do away with any age-graded ministry: minister to families as a whole and include children in adult activities. They make the case that the Bible doesn't talk about teens, and in Bible times people were classified as adults by the time they were thirteen. They say that the reason teens rebel and have the problems inherent to those years is that we have created a new category between children and adults, and student ministries reinforce the problem.

While I personally disagree, Voddie Baucham, one of today's most popular and gifted Christian communicators, teaches this elimination of student ministry. He makes a strong statement on his website blog: "Let me be clear... there is no such thing as 'Biblical' youth ministry."[14] Others agree with him. Vision Forum Ministries is a major influence of hundreds of family-integrated churches. The following excerpt from the organization's website states,

Today, the primary method for training Christian young

people is the modern Sunday school structure... Yet this structure cannot be found anywhere in the Bible. It is not commanded in Scripture. It is not demonstrated in Scripture. Our modern method for training children has no basis in God's Word.[15]

The organization continues,

If we look at Scripture alone, we must conclude that God's way of teaching children is through the engagement of fathers and through the preaching ("kerusso") of qualified teachers within the context of the church.[16]

Vision Forum Ministries says the only two biblical ways to disciple children are teaching by parents and preaching. Their solution? Stop age-graded ministries such as student ministry and keep families together at all times. I question that logic because of two specific passages in Scripture. First, Luke 2:46 shows Christ sitting in the midst of rabbis or teachers (the word "kerusso" is not used) listening to them and talking to them, a practice common in those days. Second, Galatians 3:24 alludes to the Hebrew idea of a tutor, instructor, or schoolmaster (related to the word "paideia," which cannot mean to preach and never refers to a parent). Rabbis would teach in the synagogues in Talmud and Mishnah schooling, which were teaching for different aged children. The point I want to make is that more than parental teaching and preaching was involved in the process, which is different than what Vision Forum would suggest. Sure it was called Mishnah school then (which was age-graded), and we call it Sunday School or Teen Bible Study now. However, the concept is the same—there is biblical precedent for age-graded ministries and for parents allowing non-family members to teach their children.

Others also see age-graded ministries as the problem. One homeschooling publication published an article entitled "Church and Family or Church vs. Family," which said,

> Sadly the groundwork for this erosion and exodus of the faith for many young people was often laid in the very place considered a haven for the spiritual growth of children—the age-segregated church structure and youth programming.[17]

Some critics have begun to call this family-only thinking "hyperfamilism" because the movement believes the church should spend all its time enriching family life and no time meeting other needs or providing other ministries.[18] Others warn about hyperfamilism becoming a "virtual idolatry of the home" and are afraid that it will "jeopardize the church's larger task of evangelism."[19]

There is much talk about "church versus family," a phrase that makes me uncomfortable. There are a growing and vocal few that have swung the pendulum to the extreme to suggest we abolish student and children's ministry, but others go to the other far extreme and say that student ministry is better off with no parent involvement. Mike Yaconelli, founder of

Youth Specialties, wrote an article entitled "The Problem of
Parents," in which he points to the countless problems parents cause:

> What's the biggest obstacle to effective youth ministry?
> Parents... There just aren't very many families doing it,
> which is why youth ministry is so very important; but,
> to be honest, family ministry isn't biblical anyway...
> Jesus himself told his disciples that he'd be the reason
> families break up.[20]

Let's all be cautious of anyone that would insist on
championing one institution at the demise of the other. God
gave us the two institutions, so we cannot ignore one in favor
of another. We must identify a middle ground between these
extreme views and recover a biblical framework for student
ministry. So, do we really need the second institution? What
is the role of the church, if any? Should we stop age-graded
ministry? This section will answer those questions. It will
provide a biblical understanding of why the church and its
student ministries exist and what its role in this world is.

While we often talk about church, Jesus only directly
spoke of it two times. In Matthew 16:15-18 Jesus talked with
His disciples and asked,

> "Who do you say I am?" Simon Peter answered, "You
> are the Christ, the Son of the living God." Jesus replied,
> "Blessed are you, Simon son of Jonah, for this was not

revealed to you by man, but by my Father in heaven.
And I tell you that you are Peter, and on this rock I
will build my church, and the gates of Hades will not
overcome it."

As Jesus spoke of the church, He also offered a promise: nothing, not even hell itself, will be able to overcome the church. While we all can see ominous signs, Jesus' promise should encourage us that He will continue to fight for the church and protect it. This passage reveals to us the importance Jesus placed on the coming church.

While Jesus' words promised the church was coming, its beginning was carefully chronicled for us in Acts 2. It is important to note that the beginning of the church was marked with miracles, speaking in foreign languages and thousands of salvations. This is important because God started the church, not the disciples. The church was ordained by God and given an important role on earth and for eternity. Also, notice what the start of the church was like at the end of Acts 2:

They devoted themselves to the apostles' teaching
and to the fellowship, to the breaking of bread and to
prayer. Everyone was filled with awe, and many wonders and miraculous signs were done by the apostles.
All the believers were together and had everything in
common. Selling their possessions and goods, they
gave to anyone as he had need. Every day they continued to meet together in the temple courts. They broke

> bread in their homes and ate together with glad and
> sincere hearts, praising God and enjoying the favor
> of all the people. And the Lord added to their number
> daily those who were being saved (vv. 42-47).

Notice the relationship between home and church; there was no division between the two. What happened in church moved into the home and vice versa. And what was the result? The Lord blessed, and people were saved. Sadly, the two have drifted apart, and our current model of student ministry now accepts, if not promotes, the division. Maybe we have lost what the church understood two thousand years ago—its vital role of supporting and championing the family. The Bible has more to say about the church:

> Consequently, you are no longer foreigners and aliens,
> but fellow citizens with God's people and members of
> God's household.... And in him you too are being built
> together to become a dwelling in which God lives by
> his Spirit (Ephesians 2:19, 22).

It is interesting how God describes the second institution in terms of the first, which begs the question: If we don't fully understand the first institution, can we fully understand the second? Ephesians 5 says,

> Christ loved the church and gave himself up for her
> to make her holy, cleansing her by the washing with

water through the word, and to present her to himself as a radiant church, without stain or wrinkle or any other blemish, but holy and blameless.... He feeds and cares for it, just as Christ does the church—for we are members of his body (vv. 25-27, 28-30).

God passionately loves the church like a groom loves his bride and would die for her. This passage speaks strongly to those parents who think they can successfully raise children without a partnership with the church. Once again, God designed the two institutions to work together. First Corinthians 12:14-20 says,

Now the body is not made up of one part but of many. If the foot should say, "Because I am not a hand, I do not belong to the body," it would not for that reason cease to be part of the body. And if the ear should say, "Because I am not an eye, I do not belong to the body," it would not for that reason cease to be part of the body. If the whole body were an eye, where would the sense of hearing be? If the whole body were an ear, where would the sense of smell be? But in fact God has arranged the parts in the body, every one of them, just as he wanted them to be. If they were all one part, where would the body be? As it is, there are many parts, but one body.

This is a powerful picture of the church—a group of individuals and families working together for the same purpose: to glorify God. There is no place for turfism in the church; instead the goal is for each part—pastor, parent, student, anyone—to support others and their roles in the Body. The message is one of cooperation, partnership, and interdependence.

WHAT'S THE PURPOSE?

The church is an important part of God's plan, just as the family is. God loves the church and ordained it with several purposes, and those purposes are defined differently in the scriptures than those for the family. There is a need for the church; it accomplishes things that the family does not. Extremists who want to eliminate student ministry have not seen how it can work when it is in partnership, rather than competition, with the family. It can champion the family like no other institution on earth can. So what are the biblically assigned purposes for the church and for student ministry? You could express the church's purposes in several ways, but our church uses three words: exalt, edify, and evangelize. Here's how the Bible says it.

PURPOSE: EXALTATION

- Exaltation is found in Matthew 22:37-38 as Jesus says, "Love the Lord your God with all your heart and with all your soul and with all your mind. This is the first and greatest commandment."
- It is also clearly seen in John 4:23-24: "Yet a time is

coming and has now come when the true worshipers
will worship the Father in spirit and truth, for they are
the kind of worshipers the Father seeks. God is spirit,
and his worshipers must worship in spirit and in truth."

Churches have worship services, teen worship bands,
classes on worship, children's worship, etc. Why? Because a
primary purpose of the church is to worship God. To champion the church means to understand its primary purpose is
to glorify God. John MacArthur says, "It is absolutely essential for the church to see itself as the institution established for the glory of God. The church has been reduced from an organism that emphasizes knowing and glorifying God to an organization that focuses on man's needs."[21]

> There is a need for the church; it accomplishes things that the family does not. Extremists who want to eliminate student ministry have not seen how it can work when it is in partnership, rather than competition, with the family.

Let me be clear, by exaltation I am talking about corporate worship, our need to worship together, and the biblical mandate for the church to provide it. As has been clearly demonstrated, there is an important place for family and individual worship; we encourage that wholeheartedly. However, just family worship alone is not enough; families need the church and need the corporate worship it provides. There is power when the body of Christ comes together in worship and exalts God as one. Families cannot duplicate the powerful worship experiences that churches offer every Sunday. Too many people see worship as compartmentalized, something you do in certain places or on certain days. When students see worship at home, at church, on the road, when we lie down, when we get up (as Deuteronomy 6 says), with mom, with dad, with other adults, with other students, etc., they fully understand exaltation.

PURPOSE: EDIFICATION

Our second purpose is edification. Here's how Hebrews 10:25 puts it:

> Let us not give up meeting together, as some are in the habit of doing, but let us encourage one another—and all the more as you see the Day approaching.

David Horner, our pastor, explains edification this way:

> A significant part of the edification process of the local church is to encourage the development of a strong, Christ-centered, warm family life for every family represented in the body. Because so much of our lives is impacted by what happens within the framework of the nuclear family, the Church must be committed to

providing the kind of support and instruction needed to help its people function biblically as families. As families are disintegrating in every other level of our culture, the Church should be able to stand up and declare that in Christ Jesus, family life can be different! Unfortunately, the Church has conceded too much ground here. We must recapture what the enemy has stolen and equip the nuclear families within the family of God with the weapons of spiritual warfare to defend themselves.[22]

By edification, we are talking about encouraging, instructing, caring, teaching, and equipping all people to help them mature in Christ. Ephesians 4:11-13 puts it best:

It was he who gave some to be apostles, some to be prophets, some to be evangelists, and some to be pastors and teachers, to prepare God's people for works of service, so that the body of Christ may be built up until we all reach unity in the faith and in the knowledge of the Son of God and become mature, attaining to the whole measure of the fullness of Christ.

I know some student pastors who like to call themselves "student equippers," and while this idea is clearly depicted in this passage, notice who it actually instructs us to equip: the body of Christ. That would include not only the teens but their parents as well. Our job is to equip all of God's people with the tools they need to impact their families, their community, and the world for Christ. Families cannot do that themselves; they need other Christians in the church to lock arms with them and provide all they need to make a difference for Christ. George Barna says,

> Unlike parents who embrace the "dump and run" strategy of spiritual nurturing – dump the kids at church, run off until the allotted time has expired, then wait until next week to repeat the process to provide their offspring with their dose of spiritual experience – revolutionary parents see their church as an invaluable partner in a long-term effort to raise a mature follower of Christ.[23]

It is easy to understand the church's responsibility to disciple adults, but notice that both institutions have been assigned the task to disciple teens. Why the overlap? Those of you who know teenagers well can see God's wisdom in that plan. As stated previously, it is clear that the primary task of discipling teens falls on parents, and I believe the church must assume a supporting role. However, I am not suggesting we abolish student ministry. Quite the opposite; I believe it has an important role in teenagers' lives. Although the list could fill up a chapter, here are a few reasons why the church and its student ministries are needed:

• The church is needed to surround students with godly adults who can provide love, care, truth they can build their lives on, and a model to follow.

- The church is needed to reach out and model Christianity to teens without Christian parents.
- The church is needed to reinforce a biblical worldview to teens. We have all seen how a teen will sometimes listen to a youth volunteer or Bible study leader, even though the parent has said the same truth.
- The church is needed to be a neutral third party, serving as an impartial advisor to parents and teens.
- The church is needed to connect young people with other Christian teens who support, encourage, and hold each other accountable.
- The church is needed to provide opportunities for teens to use and sharpen their gifts, serving the Body in ways they cannot at home.

I could go on. The point is that God had wisdom in assigning specific tasks to the church, and when families and the church work together, we see a life-changing team functioning as God designed them.

PURPOSE: EVANGELISM

The third purpose of the church is evangelism. The two passages we look to are:

- Matthew 28:19-20: "Therefore go and make disciples of all nations, baptizing them in the name of the Father and of the Son and of the Holy Spirit, and teaching them to

obey everything I have commanded you. And surely I
am with you always, to the very end of the age."
• Romans 10:14-15: "How, then, can they call on the one
they have not believed in? And how can they believe
in the one of whom they have not heard? And how
can they hear without someone preaching to them?
And how can they preach unless they are sent? As it is
written, 'How beautiful are the feet of those who bring
good news!'"

Have you ever thought about how a family grows? The
easy answer is "babies being born." But in order for the new
births to come along, a family must reach outside itself. Either a new child is adopted or a family member marries an
outsider and a new child is born. If a family doesn't reach
outside itself, either it becomes extremely unhealthy, or it will
cease to exist. The same could be said about the church.

The church has an important purpose in evangelism.
There is power when the body of Christ comes together to
reach and impact the world. As people join together as a
church, as churches join together in cooperative programs,
and even as denominations reach across lines to serve alongside one another, a world-changing coalition is formed; millions of dollars fund thousands of missionaries and causes.
Families cannot duplicate a church's evangelistic and mission
efforts. As the church (and its student ministries) reaches outside itself and grows, the world is changed. You and I could
make a long list of those young people reached through the

evangelistic efforts of student ministries. We have all utilized the stat that 85 percent of people who come to Christ do so by the age of eighteen.[24] Children's and student ministries make sense because young people are open to spiritual concepts. We're foolish not to put much of our time, effort, and resources toward the group that experiences the most conversions. We would be foolish to abolish the very ministries that can help teens and their parents through the years of unparalleled turmoil and unequalled opportunity. While the biblical ideal is a partnership between parents and the church, not every student is blessed with Christian parents. It is in those cases that the church can help pick up the slack by sharing Christ and providing godly examples to follow.

> Children's and student ministries make sense because young people are open to spiritual concepts. We're foolish not to put much of our time, effort, and resources toward the group that experiences the most conversions.

Both the church and its student ministries have biblically assigned purposes: namely, exaltation, edification, and evangelism. It is interesting in passages concerning the early church, such as the aforementioned Acts 2:42, we see these three purposes functioning in perfect unison. These purposes of the church are different than the purposes of the family, which is why God ordained two institutions rather than one.

We cannot listen to the extremists who are attempting to push us to one or the other institution. It's time for the two institutions to step closer together and become partners to rescue this generation.

STUDENT MINISTRY... IN THE BEGINNING

So, why the misunderstanding of student ministry's role? Why do some people want to do away with the profession entirely? Many of these same people say this whole profession is a relatively new creation, and they are correct. It is my experience that few student pastors know how student ministry started and how it helped take us to where we are today. One might conclude that with all the efforts to keep student ministry going well that student ministry as we have come to know it is centuries old. Student ministry through the years has taken on a life of its own.

Surprising to many is the fact that the word *teenager* didn't appear in the American dictionary until the 1950s. Once the teenage block of years was widely accepted, ministries were formed to reach the new demographic (the same has happened with preteens over the past decade). Churches did not routinely hire youth ministers until the mid-1950s and early 1960s.[25] Therefore, student ministry as a profession is only a little more than fifty years old. Since its beginning, student ministry has become more specialized and more isolated. It began with teen-only classes, grew to teen-only events, and now includes teen-only worship services. The divide between families and the church has grown along with student ministry.

Many student pastors with whom I have spoken about family/church ministry framework have concerns that their student ministries have become their own entities. They also fear that there is little or no intergeneration relationships being developed among students with those of greater spiritual maturity. Al Mohler, the well-known theologian and president of Southern Seminary says, "When 'church time' is seen as a competitor to 'family time,' something is wrong at church. When family members hardly see each other at church activities, the congregation needs to take a quick inventory of its concept of ministry."[26] Holly Allen, specialist in intergenerational studies, agrees: "In the past, spending family time together and going to church were the same thing. Now, family time and church time are not compatible ideas, because families are rarely together when they are at church."[27] Are we seeking a healthy balance between keeping students together for age-appropriate settings and intergenerational ministry opportunities, or are we isolating students entirely from the rest of the church unknowingly? It would be hard to imagine that anyone would deliberately isolate students altogether from spiritual settings with adults who have walked with the Lord for years. Dr. Richard Ross fears that in the near future,

> Student ministry as a profession is only a little more than fifty years old.

Some churches will build buildings to support segregation – and they will do so with *excellence*. They
will not build for racial segregation, but to support age
segregation. Such churches will build youth centers
costing millions. Both the natural appeal of such buildings and the programming centered there will almost
guarantee teenagers will only experience church life
with people almost precisely their own age. Adults
will find no ways to bless children much less even see
them. Young people will be cut off from the richness of
almost all adult relationships. And, most importantly,
they will not see members of their own families until it
is time to meet at their car to go home.[28]

What I am saying is that student ministry is not as time-
tested as we would like to think it is. It has only been in the
recent years that we have received conclusive research on the
system we have created over the past fifty-plus years. If you
assumed that student ministry has a long, proven, successful
track record, then you may need to reconsider. The findings
suggest that the Ferrari we think we have been driving may
actually be an Edsel. The research suggests that the model
we have formed needs a change. Our survey of the topic in
the Bible also suggests that the model needs a change. Many
student pastors, many of whom are referenced on these pages, have realized that the model needs a change. There is an
agreement—it is time for a change. We must find a middle
ground between the extremes and learn how to co-champion
the family and the church in our ministries so each institution

can function as God intended.

CO-CHAMPIONING THE FAMILY AND THE CHURCH

God created the family. God created the church. And in His wisdom, He created the two to function together. The biblical ideal is one of the family supporting the church and the church supporting the family, but it's not happening today. It has reached such extremes that some parents want to stop all student ministries, and some student pastors want to stop trying to partner with parents. What God had joined together, man has separated over time.

The statistics point to a sad reality. Ten years ago researchers began to find that Christians are just as likely to divorce as non-Christians, and each year their findings have been confirmed.[29] Shouldn't the rates of Christian divorces be half as many as those from non-Christians? Or 25 percent better? Or at least 5 percent better? Sadly, they are not. If families were supported and equipped by churches, then you would think that they would make it when non-Christians without the support of Christ and the church get divorced. Christian marriages should be our brightest witness and greatest badge of distinction, but they are not. Church ministries must shift their framework to give families the tools to succeed in a society that wears down and breaks apart this institution. Eric Wallace says, "When homes and families are divided—as a matter or course—the church loses. When there is little time for church members to develop relationships around real life, the church becomes a collection of in-grown special-interest groups."[30] It is our job as student pastors to overcome the growing divide between families and the church to champion both God-given institutions equally. Or put another way:

> Programs should be church *related* and *family centered*. The task of the church is to make the whole ethos of the home evangelical in spirit and practice... The home is responsible for training children, but the church is responsible for equipping parents in how to train their children.[31]

A disconnect has formed over the past fifty years between the two institutions that were designed to work together. Sadly, it has been accepted as normal and even promoted in extreme cases. That is not a biblical framework for student ministry. The biblical ideal is the two breathing life into one another. This says it best:

> The Christian church and the Christian home as institutions are closely bound together. They are like Siamese twins: if you cut them apart you may sever an artery of life and cause one or both to die. The church cannot function as she should in a disordered world unless she employs the home as her main reliance in Christian nurture. I feel certain that the family cannot be a Christian family or a happy family unless it stays in the

circulation of those spiritual influences of which the church is the great custodian. [32]

NOTES

1 I need to thank Brian Frost for asking me this question. God used his question to begin the process that led to our restructuring student ministry and the writing of this book.

2 Tedd Tripp, *Shepherding a Child's Heart* (Wapwallopen: Shepherd Press, 1995) p.30.

3 George Barna, *Revolutionary Parenting* (Carol Stream: Tyndale House Publishers, 2007) pp.11-12.

4 Taken from familytalkonline.com/docs/AboutUs.htm.

5 Taken from www.MVParents.com.

6 Information taken from an article entitled "MTV and The Associated Press Release Landmark Study of Young People and Happiness" found at www.mtv.com/thinkmtv/research/.

7 Wayne Rice and David Veerman, *Understanding Your Teenager*, (Lakeside, CA: Understanding Your Teenager Books) p.118.

8 Christian Smith, *Soul Searching*, (Oxford University Press, 2005) p.267.

9 Mark DeVries, "The Role of Parents in Kids' Spiritual Formation," *Youth Worker Journal*, March/April 2003, p.22.

10 Taken from www.christianpost.com/article/20060510/4178.htm.

11 Eugene C. Roehlkepartain, *The Teaching Church* (Nashville: Abingdon Press, 1993), p.177.

12 Ross Campbell. *Relational Parenting* (Chicago: Moody Press, 2000). pp.136-137.

13 Josh McDowell, *The Last Christian Generation* (Holiday, FL: Green Key Books, 2006), p.60.

14 Voddie Baucham, taken from his blog at www.voddiebaucham.org/Blog/267E5D26-839E-4A82-8F9F-E050A8637544.html.

15 Scott Brown, July 21, 2005, taken from www.visionforumministries.org/issues/ uniting_church_and_family/the_sufficiency_of_scripture_a.aspx.

16 Ibid.

17 Mike and Sue Bechtel, "Church and Family or Church vs. Family" *The IAHE Informer*, May/June 2007, p.16.

18 Roy Fairchild and John Charles Wynn, *Families in the Church: A Protestant Survey* (New York: Association Press, 1961), p.16.

19 Taken from www.wlsessays.net/authors/K/KastensFamilies/KastensFamilies.rtf.

20 Mike Yaconelli, "The Problem of Parents," taken from www.youthspecialties.com/articles/Yaconelli/parents.php.

21 John MacArthur, *The Master Plan for the Church*, (Chicago: Moody Publishers, 1991) p. 25.

22 David Horner, *Firmly Rooted, Faithfully Growing: Principle Based Ministry in the Church* (2001) p. 109.

23 George Barna, p.106.

24 This stat is often quoted, and can be found, among other places, at missiology.org/mmr/mmr33.htm.

25 Mark Senter, *The Coming Revolution in Youth Ministry*, (Victor Books, 1992) p.142.

26 Al Mohler, blog dated March 14, 2007, "The New Family Trump Card- Family Time vs. Church Time." Tken from www.albertmohler.com/blog_print.php?id=899

27 Ibid.

28 Richard Ross, "Youth Ministry and the Church in Ten years," *National Network of Youth Workers Magazine*, 2006, vol.24, no.4, p.7.

29 Taken from www.barna.org/FlexPhee.aspx?Page=BarnaUpdate&BarnaUpdateId=170.

30 Eric Wallace, *Uniting Church and Home* (Solutions for Integrating Church and Home Books, 1999) p.47

31 Robert E. Clark, Joanne Brubaker, and Roy B. Zuck, *Childhood Education in the Church* (Chicago: Moody Press, 1986.) p.33.

reSHaPe:

Beginning a

Transition

The most common question we receive from churches that we work with is "Where and how do we begin?" It's a great question and one we ask ourselves regularly as God is still taking us through the process. Your process will and should look entirely different than ours. You will most likely find the change beginning with you and your understanding as you start asking difficult questions. Max Dupree wisely reminds us, "We cannot become what we need to be by remaining what we are."[1]

The goal of the current student ministry model has been to keep kids "good," out of jail, out of the back seat, and out of toxic relationships. However, it's not enough to simply help students get through the pitfalls of high school, although that is part of the assignment. The Bible clearly states our goal is to build disciples of Christ—"Therefore go and make disciples of all nations, baptizing them in the name of the Father and of the Son and of the Holy Spirit, and teaching them to obey everything I have commanded you," (Matthew 28:19). The goal for many of our ministries has become to get students to attend, when the Scriptures clearly show Christ's goal is to create disciples who reach others with the Good News of the gospel. If our ministries adopt a healthier goal, then we also must adopt different criteria for evaluating success. As previously stated, we must look for clear biblical direction and honestly evaluate our own path in light of a church culture that many times prioritizes business models over biblical principles.

> "Never be so busy ministering to everyone else's family that you lose yours."

The best place by far for all of us to start is in our own homes. John Maxwell says, "We teach what we know, but we reproduce who we are."[2] A good friend told me that a huge turning point for him and his ministry to parents came when he realized the efforts he was making to spiritually lead his family were the very ideas he needed to be sharing with the parents of his students. He would quickly tell you that he is not the perfect model, but the fact that he was making every effort at home to spiritually lead his family gave him the confidence to faithfully encourage the parents of his students to do the same.[3] Unfortunately, many pastors find themselves too drained and exhausted by the current ministry model to intentionally shepherd their own homes, which is a complete contrast to God's qualifications for a church leader. The first pastor that I served under, Dr. Tony Smith, gave me some of the best advice I have ever received: "Never be so busy ministering to everyone else's family that you lose yours." Inscribed on the tomb of an Anglican bishop in Westminster Abbey:

> When I was young and free and my imagination had no limits, I dreamed of changing the world. As I grew older and wiser, I discovered the world would not change, so I shortened my sights somewhat and decided to change only my country. But it, too, seemed immovable. As I grew into my twilight years, in one last desperate attempt, I settled for changing only my family, those closest to me, but alas, they would have none of it. And now, as I lie on my deathbed, I suddenly realize: If I had only changed myself first, then by example I would have changed my family. From their inspiration and encouragement, I would then have been able to better my country, and who knows, I may have even changed the world.[4]

Because we believe that God gave parents an incredible job assignment, it only makes sense that our future direction communicates that we are locking arms with the primary spiritual developers – parents. Josh McDowell shares that 78 percent of churched teenagers say their parents shape their attitude and actions. These studies also show that parents have three times more influence over their students than pastors or youth group leaders.[5] McDowell makes a challenging statement: "If we're going to reclaim the next generation, then the home and the church must join forces together like never before."[6] It seems that every major study being done affirms the role of parents of the truth found in Deuteronomy 6. Christian Smith says, "Contrary to popular, misguided, cultural stereotypes and frequent parental misperceptions, we believe that the evidence clearly shows that the single most important social influence on the religious and spiritual lives of adolescents is their parents. This recognition may be empowering to parents, or alarming, or both."[7] Many student pastors are waking up, in light of today's research, to the fact that it is time for a change. They realize they are losing ground and are ready to jump in, but how?

I am very encouraged by the types of questions we receive from student pastors who call or e-mail us about our ministry model. There continues to be a strong trend among churches to hire leadership who question traditional student ministry models. I have included a few e-mails representing the type of questions we receive from pastors, student pastors, and other church leaders. We will deal with many of these questions over the next few chapters.

Steve,

Johnny Derouen, Professor of Student Ministry at Southwestern Seminary in Fort Worth, Texas, recommended you and your ministry as an example of a church that is doing ministry to families well. I am currently transitioning our ministry from a student-focused perspective to a family-based, church-supported perspective. I am looking for examples to learn from in other churches engaged in similar approaches or transitions, but I have unfortunately not found many in my own area (Dallas/Fort Worth Metroplex, Texas). So Dr. Derouen recommended I contact you. Would you be willing to answer the following questions either through e-mail or over the phone?

• How would you describe the ministry model or paradigm that you are operating or implementing in your ministry?

• What are the most significant obstacles that you face in the faith development of your teenagers?

• What role do parents play in the formation, direction, and execution of your student ministry?

• How are you motivating and equipping parents to develop the faith of teenagers in your ministry?

    Josh Vaughan
    Fort Worth, TX

Steve,

- Please explain the scriptural basis/theory behind moving to parents-based ministry.
- What role does the student ministry play in shepherding and training the parents? How?
- How long did it take to move toward family-based ministry and how was it implemented (i.e., in small stages or phases, one large move, etc.)?
- What systems and structures (S&S) are in place to support this model? For example, how does the S&S of the children's and adult ministry, as well as within the student ministry, support the student ministry?
- What student ministry programs are in place to carry out this vision? (i.e., Sunday AM, midweek, small groups, etc.) and specifically how are the parents involved?
- What are the potential difficulties to look for in transitioning toward a parent-based ministry, and what were the most difficult challenges Providence faced in moving toward this model?
- What about students from broken homes, single parents, or unchurched homes where there is no parental involvement?
- What recommendations do you have in transitioning to parent-based ministry when the mindset is not parent-based?

> Andrew Pennington & Brooke Roberts
> Arlington, VA

Steve,

- How do you define Family Ministry?
- How did you implement the strategy?
- How is your vision or mission based off of your definition of Family Ministry?
- What are your main avenues or environments to accomplish this mission?
- Have you experienced a transition in this process? How did you manage the transition?
- What are some philosophical things we need to nail down before we start?
- How do you work with parents?
- How do you get parents involved?
- How do you get parents engaged?

Thanks and know that our entire educational team really looks forward to meeting with you.

Robert Kell
Johnson City, TN

As you can see, transitioning to a biblical framework is anything but simple. These e-mails point to the dozens of questions that must be answered as a ministry transitions to a biblical framework that honors families and the church. For some of you, the first three chapters may have convinced you. Now you are ready to jump in, add a bunch of new stuff onto the calendar, and get parents on your team. That is admirable but rushed. Most of the student pastors I talk to want the bottom line—programs, practices, ideas, and the outward expressions of ministry. I understand where they are coming from, but there are vital areas to consider before putting the practices in place. We must be principle driven in all we do, or we return to looking for the latest fads and gimmicks. When making any significant ministry paradigm shifts, there are four key components to consider: prayer, principles, prerequisites, and practices.

We will look in depth into each of these areas to help you better understand how and where to begin.

PRAYER

Remember Nehemiah? He was a mentor, great leader, and visionary, but there was something more about this man that brought about great change. His context really wasn't much different than ours: a culture hostile to his beliefs and a task greater than he could ever accomplish under his own strength. The following verse does not give a long list of Nehemiah's great credentials but rather describes a broken man who had a great burden: "When I heard these things, I sat down and wept. For some days I mourned and fasted and prayed" (Nehemiah 1:4). Verses 5-11 give us great insight into the first step of Nehemiah's strategy of change. Pay attention. Some of us are in his same context; we are greatly bothered by what we see bombarding today's teens, their families, and the church, and

• Prayer

• Principles

• Prerequisites

• Practices

we want to know where to start. Nehemiah began changing history the same way we can, through prayer.

We too share a similar burden with Nehemiah. Look around. Who isn't troubled by today's research? Below are several facts about the students we are trying to reach and those students in our ministries:

- Nationally, nearly one million teen girls become pregnant each year. That means close to 2,800 teens get pregnant each day.[8]
- Every 78 seconds a teen attempts suicide - every 90 seconds one succeeds.[9]
- The largest group of viewers of Internet porn is teens between ages 12 and 17.[10]
- Nearly 4 in 10 teen pregnancies (excluding those ending in miscarriages) are terminated by abortion. There were about 274,000 abortions among teens in 1996.[11]
- Of today's young people: One out of two will live in a single-parent family at some point in childhood. One in three is born to unmarried parents. One in four lives with only one parent today. One in eight is born to a teenage mother. One in twenty-five lives with neither parent.[12]
- This generation views 16 to 17 hours of television each week and sees on average 14,000 sexual scenes and references each year. Also, 42 percent of the top-selling CDs contain sexual content.[13]
- Research suggests that anywhere from 60 to 85 percent

of teens will walk away from the church after they graduate from high school.[14]

Are we weeping, or are we numb to what is happening around us? Are we mourning, or are we too busy keeping the machine going that we miss where we are headed? Does our response to this crisis resemble that of Nehemiah's? John Piper says:

Examine yourself: Does it lie within your power right now to weep over the spiritual destruction of the people on your street? Such tears come only through a profound work of God. If we want this work of God in our lives and in our churches, there will be agonizing prayer: "God, break my heart!" I choose the word "agonize" carefully.[15]

E. M. Bounds echoes the same truth: "Prayer is the language of a man burdened with a sense of need."[16] Our first response should be and must be prayer. The Scriptures implore us to pray:

• "If my people, who are called by my name, will humble themselves and pray and seek my face and turn from their wicked ways, then will I hear from heaven and will forgive their sin and will heal their land." (2 Chronicles 7:14)
• "Therefore confess your sins to each other and pray for

each other so that you may be healed. The prayer of a righteous man is powerful and effective." (James 5:16)

- "This is the confidence we have in approaching God: that if we ask anything according to his will, he hears us. And if we know that he hears us—whatever we ask—we know that we have what we asked of him." (1 John 5:14-15)
- "For the eyes of the Lord are on the righteous and his ears are attentive to their prayer." (1 Peter 3:12)

What would our students say that you and I are praying for? Is it our next event or to see God work? Is it success for our ministry or for our students' hearts and souls?

One more thing—we need to pray for God to change our hearts and to give us a depth of insight that is saturated by the principles found in His Word. John 3:30 reminds us, "He must become greater; I must become less." This means our great ideas, our church-growth gimmicks, our self-reliance, and our self-importance must decrease. Nehemiah understood the scope of the problem and that he brought nothing to the solution. He did not have the resources or finances or expertise to repair a great city; maybe that's why he wept. Nehemiah knew that God alone would have to do the work, so he prayed. Without prayer the plans you and I put into practice will not change families; God alone will have to do the work. If you want to jump into changing things without prayer, stop reading right now. Your transition will not work.

Nehemiah 9 tells us that as everyone arrived they spent a quarter of the day in Scripture reading and a quarter of the day in prayer and confession. Imagine everyone there ready to work, and there were no engineering seminars, no block-laying classes, no blueprints or architects. Nehemiah understood that his ministry was first and foremost spiritual. So they prayed, and we can learn from his example. Karl Barth rightly said, "To clasp the hands in prayer is the beginning of an uprising against the disorder of the world."[17] Prayer will fuel your change.

PRINCIPLES

Change takes time, and it must start with us. More times than not when pastors who want to implement new ideas contact us, they ask about the practices, events, and details of the programs we offer rather than the foundations that support them. Change is viewed for many as something external or programmatic, but it must be more than that. It must start with a passion inside you that is guided by biblical principles. You must be convinced that it is God's will for you to make a fundamental shift in how you think about and how you do ministry. G. K. Chesterton said, "A man is not really convinced of a philosophic theory when he finds that something proves it. He is only really convinced when he finds that everything proves it."[18] This means we first must become totally convinced on an internal level that change is necessary. Actually, the process of change doesn't begin until these biblical principles saturate us personally and then saturate our homes as we spiritually lead our families. You will probably face resistance from those who have become enticed by the bright lights of the "ministry" of busyness that screams, "It is all about you." David Wells says, "Disney is all about entertainment, and some churches have come to think that here, too, another page can be taken from its book. Entertainment has therefore emerged as a very important factor in the new mix. Ministers who resemble comedians or other entertainers are beginning to show up on church teams."[19] The break from this type of ministry starts inside your personal life and inside your team with the principles you adopt.

A friend of mine recently wrote an article for TwoInstitutions.org in which he pointed to "Sola Scriptura," the Reformation battle cry taken from a Latin term meaning "By Scripture alone."[20] Could there be a better focus to guide our ministry? God has expressed everything we need to know about ministry in His Word, meaning there is nothing more important than the biblical principles weighing heavily on our personal lives and ministries. Our senior pastor, David Horner, writes about the importance of being principle driven in his book *Firmly Rooted, Faithfully Growing*:

> If we want to serve Christ faithfully as His people, biblical principles cannot be compromised. Certain criteria based on unchanging principles are critical if a church is to serve Christ effectively. After many years of study and practice, I believe strongly that the body of Christ functions best when it understands itself as a principle-based ministry. The Church can never become what

Christ designed it to be unless its identity is based on principles discovered in the Bible, a resource given to us by God for just that purpose.[21]

Philippians 1:9 has given me much to think about over the last five years of ministry: "And this is my prayer: that your love may abound more and more in knowledge and depth of insight." Depth of insight? Look around you. Are most student ministries you are aware of spilling over from the richness of scriptural insight, or are they blown and tossed by every fad and chasing every idea they heard the church down the street is doing? How about your ministry? It's unfortunate that with many of us, our theology stopped growing the day we graduated from college or seminary. Once we hit the treadmill of ministry, our searching the Scriptures for biblical principles for ministry ended. There are simply too many plates spinning, making it difficult to take a hard look for truths that will guide us personally. Instead, the only time we may find ourselves in His Word is while we are rushing to prepare for a Wednesday night youth event.

David Wells asks, "Does the church have the courage to become relevant by becoming biblical?"[22] To avoid a shallow, event-driven, chasing-the-latest-fad student ministry, you must first decide specifically which biblical principles your team will use to build your ministry. The only way to avoid being sucked in by every gimmick at the latest student ministry megaconference is to have a clear set of defined principles and the conviction to live by them.

Many years ago the leadership at our church, Providence, defined a set of core values that both guide us and define us. I have done a similar thing for my personal ministry and my personal life. The set of principles that guide my ministry are:

1. Everything I do must honor God above all.
   (1 Corinthians 10:31)

2. We are to be biblical stewards of everything God has entrusted to us. (Matthew 6:19-21)

3. God has ordained parents as the primary disciplers of their children. (Deuteronomy 6:4-9)

4. God has ordained the church to support, equip and resource families. (Ephesians 4:12)

5. The goal of student ministry is to make disciples who seek to bring others into a relationship with Christ. (Matthew 28:19-20)

6. The three primary needs of students and adults alike are: love and care, a model to follow and truth to build their life on. (1 Peter 2:21)

7. Effective student ministry co-champions the family and the church. (Acts 2:42-47)

8. A biblical framework is always valued over cultural relevancy. Scripture alone will guide.
   (2 Timothy 3:16-17)

Let's be clear. I am not for a moment suggesting that others need to adopt my set of principles. While it is likely yours may be similar to those I have found, I would encourage you to search the Word and formulate your own. Some questions you need to answer are:

- What are the foundational scriptures you will build ministry on? (Looking back over the verses listed in Chapter 3 is a good place to start).
- What are your goals for student ministry, or how do you define success?
- What is expected from your students and their parents?
- Which students' needs will you focus on meeting?
- What will you choose to value and choose not to value?

To begin to rethink and reshape your ministry, you need clear principles that will guide you through your transition.

PREREQUISITES

Once your personal and ministry principles are established, the next step involves more prayer, patience, and groundwork. You have rethought your paradigm; your values have shifted, and you're ready to do things differently. However, your key leaders and your church aren't there yet. Your students won't understand why you're messing with things, and your church leadership may wonder what has gotten into you. There are key things that need to happen before you jump in and find yourself in over your head.

The first area to consider in this phase of your transition

is a starting point. Knowing where you are now is just as important, if not more so, than where you are going. You cannot get correct directions from Point A to Point B, not even on MapQuest, without the prerequisite of a starting location. Therefore, know where you are starting.

Our ministry staff and our Discovery Team (which included youth workers, six parent couples, a single mom, and a few students) walked through a process to help us discover where we were as a ministry. We discussed what the drivers and restrainers were as we continued our transition. Drivers are clear statements of where we are going and what ministry should look like. Restrainers are where we are now and what could be holding us back. Our list looked like this:

Drivers:

- Prayer- Is everything we do being supported in prayer as we would desire?
- God's Word- Is our ministry functioning from a biblical framework?
- Holy Spirit- Do we sense that God is leading and working in all facets of our ministry?
- Parents- Are we exhorting parents in their proper role of disciplers?
- Contribution- Are our parents contributors more than consumers in our ministry?
- Unity- Do the parents, leaders, church, and students all understand the heartbeat of our ministry?
- Vision casting- Are we helping students and parents

understand the benefits of following God's plan for families?

- Communication- What avenues are in place for communication?
- Training- How do we maximize events that train parents?

Restrainers:

- Parents and students who are just looking for fun
- Unhealthy expectations
- Satan
- Parents who prefer the church do it all
- Unchartered water
- Resources
- The lack of models to look to for guidance
- Changing minds
- Overwhelmed leaders
- Unequipped/unprepared leaders

Once we worked through the lists, we began to develop a glimpse of our next steps. Again, your list probably will be different than ours, so your next steps may be as well. Regardless, the following are eight prerequisites all ministries must face to begin a transition to rethink and reshape themselves.

1) Pray.

Maybe you're thinking, "Didn't we already cover this?" Yes, but prayer is that important. This kind of shift cannot be fueled by our efforts alone. Pray for change in your own life and family before you plan to bring about change in the families of your teens. Ask God to work in your heart so that your family is ministered to first as you honor them by making them your ministry priority. As a result you will be able to minister to others out of the overflow of what God is doing in your family. I pray every day that God will give me insight into His Word as I seek His guidance in leading my family. I want to be a blessing to my wife, Tina, each day. I do not want her to feel she receives the leftovers of my ministry efforts. I want my children – Sara, William and Tyler – to know that my church ministry doesn't come close to my priority and joy of spending time with them. It is only through the supernatural work of God that I am consistently able to keep my family as my clear first priority. Remember that this new message will never be received and embraced by your students and their parents if it is not true and active in your life personally.

> **Remember that this new message will never be received and embraced by your students and their parents if it is not true and active in your life personally.**

2) Lead with biblical conviction.

There will be a day when you will be challenged. You

will be asked, "Why?" "What's wrong with the way we've always done it?" "Are you saying that we were wrong for all those years?" Do you know what your answer will be? One of the most uncomfortable positions to ever be in is one where we have very few answers. We should never move forward until we are fully persuaded from God's Word that our ministries must honor the two institutions that He has given us. People look to you as a spiritual leader with a word from God. When we lead with conviction and confidence that comes from time spent in prayer and Bible study, people see that and are glad to follow.

The above questions should be easy to answer when we think of them in the following terms. First, we believe that the biblical model of student ministry points to parents as the primary disciplers of their children, and the church has a critical role of partnering with and equipping those parents. Second, we know that research clearly shows us that the current model of student ministry isn't accomplishing what we thought it was. Third, many of us have been doing this long enough to see that the old way of thinking is failing students and parents and causing our students to graduate from God. I can say with biblical conviction that transitioning to a biblical model of student ministry is God-honoring, healthier for families, and better for students, and when this transition happens the church is strengthened.

3) Secure support of leadership.

Pastors, church leaders, and student pastors must be on

the same page in their understanding of the role of parents and the role of the church. Because we lead from the middle of the pack we must proceed only when we are fully supported and backed by the church leadership. The church glorifies God best when it moves in unison, and its work is greatly enhanced by the willingness of its members to serve together. I would never begin a process of change in any way without the full support of those God has placed in leadership over my life. God has placed those I work under as an umbrella of protection for my life, my family, and my ministry. As we have moved forward with their direction, blessing, and encouragement, our ministry has been sharpened by their wisdom, discernment, and contributions, and buy-in from the church has been enhanced.

I love Isaiah 30:21: "Whether you turn to the right or to the left, your ears will hear a voice behind you, saying, 'This is the way; walk in it.'" The context is talking about the people hearing teachers who tell them which way is God's way. This can never happen in student ministry if our leadership is not on the same page. In some churches a leader may say, "This is the way," while another argues, "No, this is." We need to have a unified voice as leaders, knowing God's will and clearly communicating His plan to people.

Our pastoral team at Providence met early in the transition process. Our senior pastor and my supervising pastor provided vision, crucial direction, and leadership as we began thinking through our transition. I then began talking with our student ministry staff. Along the way, I spent time with our children's pastor, college pastors, adult education pastor, etc. My view and burden for family ministry were stretched even further because of the time spent with these men. Your staff is different than ours, so you may need to meet with different people. Regardless of who you meet with, I can assure you that a successful transition will not happen without the support from your leadership.

> Remember that it isn't your job to personally convince every parent they must disciple their children; that is God's job while you continue to present the truth of God's Word.

4) Be realistic.

Change takes time, and this transition may take years; therefore, a long-term commitment is required from everyone. Remember that it isn't your job to personally convince every parent they must disciple their children; that is God's job while you continue to present the truth of God's Word. Our experience has been that God is faithful to honor His Word. One of Providence's core values is "Faithfulness over Fruitfulness," meaning it is our job to faithfully teach and serve, even if the fruit isn't quickly seen. This has created a very healthy environment that gives great freedom to the church and its leaders to take God at His word and leave the eternal results in His hands.

I encourage you to be very realistic in the process, which means you should not expect instant results. Be faithful to God's Word, and leave the results in God's hands. If the first thing you tackle is family worship, and 25 percent of families begin having devotions the first year, be thrilled; that's likely many more than did so last year and many more than the average student ministry in the country. A realistic way we tackled things was to take the time to restructure one grade level each year. Realistic, attainable goals can give you the momentum you need to continue your transition.

5) Understand your church's culture.

How do your church members define a successful student ministry? What role do your church members feel they play in the spiritual discipleship of their students? Some might answer this question by saying, "We pay a student pastor." Your church may be full of good teachers who are comfortable with family worship or full of parents who are scared to death at the thought. Your church may be full of mature believers who just need some encouragement or full of first-generation Christians who have never heard that it is their responsibility to lead their children. Just as it is important for our missionaries to understand their ministry culture, we also need to understand our ministry culture and learn the best way to reach those in it.

Jesus gave us some wisdom saying, "Suppose one of you wants to build a tower. Will he not first sit down and estimate the cost to see if he has enough money to complete it?" (Luke 14:28). We have to count the cost before we jump in over our heads. Take time to study your church culture, so you'll know how to better equip parents.

6) Ask the tough questions.

The following are a few questions we addressed:

- Can I honestly say I have bathed this transition in prayer?
- Can I winsomely articulate a biblical position of student ministry?
- What are the major hurdles that our leadership team can identify?
- Am I committed to staying at my church long enough to see these changes through?
- What is my church's position on student ministry?
- How many families do any form of Bible teaching at home?
- What does the leadership really want to see happen?
- How much time have I personally spent to find depth of insight through studying God's Word?
- Where are the students who graduated from this ministry five years ago? Are they serving in the church?

Fifteen years ago I was asked to speak at a student ministry conference in my hometown where I first served. Before my first session, a young lady who had been in my ministry years ago served me at a local restaurant. I could tell she wasn't doing well, and I asked her if she was still in church. She said, "I quit going to church shortly after you left as student pastor because church wasn't fun anymore." While she may have meant it as a compliment, it was anything but. I walked away asking myself some really tough questions and wondered if my ministry was more fun than substance. Did I really make the impact that I had hoped to? You may be surprised how real answers to tough questions will lead you, as they have me over the years, to make necessary changes.

7) Start slowly and lead intentionally.

I can't stress this enough. Anyone who makes sweeping changes without laying the groundwork is asking for trouble. I would encourage a year-by-year approach that begins with your middle-schoolers and their parents. It is important to remember that when you begin you should do it right and not get sloppy in your haste.

An important step in the process is conversations—lots of conversations. We had lunch with people, invited families over for dinner, met for coffee, had staff meetings, met with our Parent Leadership Team (PLT), and met with our Discovery Team. These conversations continue today. The transition to this type of ministry will fill up your calendar in a whole new way. The conversations are both times for teaching and for listening. You should be able to explain a biblical model of student ministry, taking them to the Scriptures. You should also be able to lay out the facts of how the current way of thinking isn't accomplishing what we thought it was. In addition, you should be able to listen to the people you have been called to shepherd, learning how you can equip them for their job of discipling their teens. We must value the contributions of those who entrusted you and me with ministry to their children.

Five Conversations You Must Have:
- Meet with your senior pastor.
- Meet with your church leadership, elders, or deacons.
- Meet with your key ministry leaders and volunteers.
- Meet with your most vocal, loyal, and influential parents of students.
- Meet with key student leaders or youth council.

If you start to encounter significant resistance, then you likely moved too quickly and need to go back to the beginning – praying, teaching, and meeting with key people. If your key people are on board, then they can help you continue the transition.

8) Recruit a Parent Leadership Team.

The greatest advocates of our ministry approach are by far our parents. We constantly work with our parents and allow them to help shape our ministry because we value their contribution and their creative ideas; it only makes sense that we need their input if our ministry is to be seen as an extension of their ministry. Working with parents in this type of partnership is a continual process as we seek greater ways to partner with them. Also, we regularly ask our parent teams what a student ministry would look like built on biblical principles. These teams are a huge blessing because they cast vision, recruit leaders, serve as advocates, and help pave the way for future ministry direction. You cannot be the only one who can articulate a biblical position for your ministry.

We formed our PLT several years ago with one purpose in mind: to lock arms with a group of parents who will help us rethink what we are doing. We were careful with our selections. These parents became our most vocal supporters because they knew our hearts and what we hoped to accomplish regarding the transition. They were able to speak with confidence and silence the critics who had made faulty assumptions. And they were able to give us an insider's perspective on how to make this transition as successful as possible for other parents.

PRACTICES

Once you have made prayer a continuous part of the process, clearly defined and shared your principles with your team, and covered all prerequisites, it is then time to start putting things in place. This is the most fun and easiest part to me. This is when you start dreaming. As we have said several times, the key is to move slowly. This is no sprint. The idea is to start a pace you can sustain for years to come. The change isn't like the ones hyped at youth ministry conferences because it is a fundamental rethinking of how you define ministry, rather than a few ideas to pepper into your appointment book or squeeze into your Wednesday night talk. This isn't about adding new activities to an already overcrowded calendar but rather a streamlined approach that enables you to clear the calendar so you aren't competing with families or the church. Bigger really isn't better. In *Simple Church*, Thom Rainer speaks of the type of focus that is needed as he challenges church leaders to "say no to almost everything, eliminate and limit adding."[23] When Jack Welch became the CEO of General Electric, he made some bold statements. He said that GE would be number one or number two in every market, or they would eliminate that part of the business. They would focus only where they could be the best; they would say no to everything else.[24] This approach is catching on in ministries as many pastors and staff are now seeking a more streamlined and targeted approach to ministry.

> In thirteen years of ministry I had never been asked to stop doing anything. Never. How freeing. I learned that less can be more.

After eight months of being on the job at Providence and attending my first staff retreat, I felt the pressure to suggest a new idea to remind the pastors what a good decision they made when they hired me. I can't recall what my idea was, but I will never forget my senior pastor asking me what we would eliminate in order to begin this new endeavor. In thirteen years of ministry I had never been asked to stop doing anything. Never. How freeing. I learned that less can be more.

At Providence, this process of change began slowly as we sought to do it well and strategically. Each year we focused on a grade at a time rather than revamping the entire student ministry in a year. The idea was to start slowly and keep a pace that was sustainable. Our first new ministry effort was aimed toward sixth-grade students and their parents. "Bridge 57" bridges the years between fifth and seventh grades and from Children's Ministries to Student Ministries. Our desire was to engage parents and their children as part of our strategy to minister to and with families. Every event planned for our sixth graders is aimed at both parent and child. Typical events might include; Father/Son Paintball, Father/Daughter Date Night, Mother/Daughter Overnight Getaway, Father/Son Overnight or a Mother/Son Chili Cook-off. Our hope is that parents understand our very strong desire to have them involved in our ministry and that we consider them vital ministry partners. Someone once said, "It takes two to tango," and just as parents want us to play an important role in the spiritual development of their children, we want our parents to know that we need their involvement for ministry to their students to be effective. They have to understand that Providence Student Ministries refuses to accept the current mentality of church being a spiritual drop-off service. Looking back, it was a busy year as we changed the culture of sixth-grade ministry, but it prepared us for future changes.

We started Passage 7 for our seventh graders and their parents after we had one year of Bridge 57 under our belt. We began this ministry at the same time we were evaluating our successes and mistakes of Bridge 57. There are two parent-driven objectives for our Passage 7 ministry. The first objective is for parents to journal to their child—throughout a yearlong process—their prayers, memories, encouragement, values, life skills, and dreams. The second objective for the seventh-grade year is for parents and students to plan a passage trip together. More details about these programs are in the next chapters.

Although we continue to add new elements each year, some ministry elements we have already implemented include:

- The RTI Strategy: Resource, Train, Involve Parents
- Parent Leadership Team
- Discovery Team
- Parent training sessions
- Summit 8 - Eighth-grade ministry
- 15 by 15 - Fifteen values we instill in our students by age fifteen
- 7-Year Curriculum Map
- Journey Day
- Family Worship Plan

- Read-through-the-Bible Family/Student Plan
- Passage Trip
- Passage Journal

In the remaining chapters we will discuss several of the practices mentioned above, specific programs and systems we have put in place, and ideas to help you in your transition.

A CHANGE OF MIND

I had supper once with two friends and their wives. Both of these guys lead ministries that are among the largest student ministries in the country, and both seek to encourage their parents as primary disciplers. One of them paused about two hours into our conversation and looked at me and said, "Steve, you are talking about a new way of thinking, not a few creative ideas to periodically throw the parents a bone." Exactly. A transition like this doesn't start by adding new programs to your calendar or in creative topics for your Wednesday night talks. This transition starts in your head, as you find new principles to guide your ministry. It starts on your knees, as you pray for clear direction from God. It starts in your heart, as you become passionate about a different set of values. It starts in your family, as you work toward a lasting spiritual legacy. This kind of transition starts within you, as you rethink and reshape your ministry to reflect a biblical model for student ministry. If you're ready for a change, it has to start in you.

NOTES

1 Max Dupree, taken from www.leadership-tools.com/famous-quote-people.html.

2 John Maxwell, taken from www.naspleadership.com/about.php

3 Thanks to Steve Brown, student pastor at the Church at the Park in Durham, NC.

4 Taken from www.giveitforwardtoday.org/index.php?page=stories.

5 Josh McDowell, *The Last Christian Generation* (Holiday, FL: Green Key Books, 2006), p.59.

6 Ibid., p.60.

7 Christian Smith, *Soul Searching*, (Oxford University Press, 2005) p.261.

8 "Facts in Brief: Teen Sex and Pregnancy" (New York, The Alan Guttmacher Institute, 1996).

9 National Center for Health Statistics, taken from www.cdc.gov/nchs/.

10 Family Safe Media, December 15, 2005, taken from www.children-online.org/frames/research.html.

11 Information taken from www.childbirthsolutions.com/articles/pregnancy/teensex/index.php.

12 The State of America's Children, 1998 Yearbook, Children's Defense Fund.

13 Information taken from http://battlecry.com/pages/magnitude.php.

14 Josh McDowell, *The Last Christian Generation*; David Wheaton, *University of Destruction*; George Barna, *Real Teens*; Ron Luce, *Battle Cry for a Generation*, and others as presented in the research in Chapter 1.

15 John Piper, *Brothers, We Are Not Professionals* (Nashville, Broadman & Holman, 2002) pp.56-57.

16 E. M. Bounds, taken from www.thinkexist/quotes/e._m._bounds/.

17 Karl Barth, taken from en.wikiquote.org/wiki/Karl_Barth.

18 G. K. Chesterton, Orthodoxy, Public Domain.

19 David Wells, *Above All Earthly Pow'rs* (Eerdmans Publishing, 2005) p.273.

20 Taken from www.twoinstitutions.org.

21 David Horner, *Firmly Rooted, Faithfully Growing–Principle-Based Ministry in the Church*, p.21.

22 David Wells, *Losing Our Virtue* (Eerdmans Publishing, 1999) p.199.

23 Thom Rainer, *Simple Church* (Nashville, Broadman & Holman, 2006) p.197.

24 Ibid., p.226.

resource:

Locking

Arms with

Parents

Partnership with parents; it sounds simpler than it is. You may be convinced that it's time to partner with the families of your teens, but are they convinced? Sadly, many are convinced otherwise. Ten things I have heard said by parents are:

- "I can't disciple, because I've never been disciped myself."
- "We pay the youth pastor to do that."
- "I'm just not a teacher."
- "I don't know the Bible and can't answer their questions."
- "My kids won't listen to me."
- "It's too late; I would start this if I'd

known about it before my kid became a teenager."
- "We're not cool enough to relate to our kids; the youth pastor does that better."
- "I'm too busy providing for my kids' needs; I bring them to church to take care of their spiritual needs."
- "I'm not qualified; I've never been to seminary."
- "You're right; it is my responsibility. Can you help me get started?"

For many parents the thought of discipling their teenagers seems daunting. Not only does society encourage parents to leave education to the professionals, but the church unknowingly does the same by neglecting to teach scriptural mentoring principles to parents. Parents, pastors, and teens have come to accept a model that isn't biblical and doesn't work. As you read through the list above, you likely recognized several comments yourself, but perhaps the scariest item on the list for most student pastors is the last one. We are used to doing it ourselves, but when asked to show a parent how to do it, we may be the ones making excuses.

Things haven't always been this way. The Hebrew model taught (and continues to teach) parents that it is their responsibility to disciple. Deuteronomy 4:9 says, "Only be careful, and watch yourselves closely so that you do not forget the things your eyes have seen or let them slip from your heart as long as you live. Teach them to your children and to their children after them." Jewish parents understood and still understand the goal of parenting is to shepherd their children toward God. However, today our culture presents a different view, which assumes only trained pastors are equipped to teach children.

One phrase that a few critical (and vocal) parents like to throw the way of student pastors is, "My child isn't getting enough meat in your program." That one stings. Here we are, trying to faithfully teach the Word, and they are in effect telling us that we are failing. Most of us usually brush off their criticism, reminding ourselves that they are critical of anything that seems lighthearted or fun, and they think that youth meetings need to be an hour of reading the KJV. Instead of dismissing their comments, think about the criticism, which reveals a faulty perspective. Nowhere in Scripture does it teach that it is the church's responsibility to be the exclusive disciplers. If their child isn't getting "meat," then they need to look no further than their kitchen table. (You may want to remind those parents of that the next time that shot is lobbed into your court). While our desire is to provide "meat" every chance we can—to teach systematic theology, discuss complex ethical issues, help teens wrestle with the questions of the faith, look at church history, etc.—our overall objective is to present truth that nourishes everyone, from the new Christian to the long-time believer. We are not the exclusive "meat" givers; parents primarily own that task. Our charge is to resource, train, and involve parents—as well as echo their teaching—as they present the truth to their teens.

The one mistake the church can never make is to try to adjust the biblical role that parents have been clearly given.

Even if parents are abdicating their role, we should never be content to take it. I have heard parents make the ten statements above as if they were some type of loophole for accepting a ministry model that continues to foster a spiritual drop-off service and encourages sidelined parents. I've heard student pastors talk about busy families who aren't discipling their teens and have resolved in their mind that they will take on the spiritual responsibility for dozens of teens. It's like a person throwing their hands in the air saying, "Well if you won't do it then I guess I'll have to." The harsh reality is, however, when youth pastors are handed all the spiritual responsibility, teens graduate from God when they graduate from student ministry. We cannot adjust God's design to make it easier on everyone involved. What's next? Should we also stop taking up an offering because some families don't give? Should we stop serving the Lord's Supper because some take it without a clean conscience? We cannot adjust the mandate in the Scriptures because some people think this biblical framework doesn't fit today's families. Instead, we must adjust our ministry models and way of thinking to align with the truth

> The harsh reality is, however, when youth pastors are handed all the spiritual responsibility, teens graduate from God when they graduate from student ministry.

presented in God's Word. Bruce Wilkinson points to the biblical model saying, "Whether parents intend this or not, the home is the single most powerful arena on earth to change a life for God."[1]

> The one mistake the church can never make is to try to adjust the biblical role that parents have been clearly given. Even if parents are abdicating their role, we should never be content to take it.

WHY WE NEED A CHANGE

Equipping parents to lead their families, allowing parents to influence our ministries and making sure our parents don't see church as a drop-off service requires intentional effort. As we began to work through this transition, we found we needed a process to make sure parents are elevated to their place of importance. We have identified five areas that support why churches must be intentional about restoring parents to their rightful place as primary disciplers and areas you should consider before deciding on your student ministry's future direction.

1) Biblical mandate

You have likely read about Deuteronomy 6 enough in these pages to have it memorized, but that passage, along with others mentioned, is foundational for a biblical understanding of student ministry. Steve Farrar talks about the mandate in Deuteronomy 6 and other passages, saying, "There is no 'new and improved' version to these commands. They have not been upgraded. They were perfect when they were given and they will be perfect for as long as men walk the earth... The job description is timeless."[2] The Bible is unmistakably clear that it is the parents' job to disciple their children. But there is another place to look; one you likely often flip past—the genealogies.

> They understood that their family and their faith affected more than mom, dad, brother, and sister. More than the here and now, faith affects generations.

Reading about genealogies in a student ministry book may seem strange, but genealogies are in the Bible for a reason. There are dozens of names and "begats" in the Scriptures, but have you ever stopped and considered why? We find it hard to read a genealogy because it covers pages of names we don't know and can't pronounce, and because it's not about our family. However, Jesus likely saw the list in Luke 3 differently than we do today. He knew the story of Tamar's struggles. He could tell you about Rahab's courage. He was very familiar with David's faith. He understood the godly legacy left to Him by these heroes of the faith. Each name was an epic story of God being faithful to family. The problem is that we don't see these lists like those in a Hebrew model would. They understood that their family and their faith affected more than mom, dad, brother, and sister. More than the here and now, faith affects generations.

Many never think about generational parenting. Most don't think about a lasting legacy for Christ. Some parents think that they have eighteen to twenty years in this parenting thing and they're done. Maybe you've seen the Mercedes commercial that illustrates our current cultural view. It says, "3,212 conference calls, 745 airplane trips, 1,000 hours of lost sleep, two out of three kids raised successfully... it's payback time: The new E-class Mercedes." Where we think that two out of three aren't bad results in child rearing, those in the Hebrew model thought that two out of three meant that dozens of descendants would be left without a spiritual heritage. This Hebrew concept of generational parenting can be seen as early as Abraham.

- We see in Genesis 18:19 that Abraham understood his clear God-given assignment: "I have chosen him, so that he will direct his children and his *household after him* to keep the way of the LORD by doing what is right and just."

Other places we see a multi-generational perspective:
- Psalm 119:90 says, "Your faithfulness continues through all *generations*; you established the earth, and it endures."

- Psalm 89:4 says, "I will establish your line forever and make your throne firm through all *generations*."
- Joshua 22:27 says, "On the contrary, it is to be a witness between us and you and the *generations* that follow, that we will worship the LORD at his sanctuary with our burnt offerings, sacrifices and fellowship offerings. Then in the future your *descendants* will not be able to say to ours, 'You have no share in the LORD.'"
- Isaiah 60:15 says, "Although you have been forsaken and hated, with no one traveling through, I will make you the everlasting pride and the joy of all *generations*."

What if the church understood and taught about this powerful influence and equipped parents for a generational legacy? What if our children and their children and their children knew the spiritual heritage of families who passed down their faith to each generation? The first fact we must consider is the biblical principle of parents being the primary disciplers to pass down the faith. The church cannot afford to yawn passively when today's studies reveal that we are losing so many of our own children.

2) State of today's families

Another reason we must implement a system to resource, train, and involve parents is the fact that today's families are under attack and have few places to go for help. Dr. Richard Land writes, "Recent studies show virtually no difference between the divorce rate of Christians and the general population."[3] Less than half of our youth grow up in a house with mom and dad both present, and more than a million children a year watch their parents divorce.[4] Amazingly 15 percent of Protestant senior pastors have been divorced.[5] The Council on Families in America stated, "Our nation has largely shifted from a culture of marriage to a culture of divorce. Once we were a nation in which a strong marriage was seen as the best route to achieving the American dream. We have now become a nation in which divorce is commonly seen as the path to personal liberation."[6] Not only should the prevalence of divorce alarm us, but the acceptance of it should as well. It is time for the church to refuse to accept the current divorce rate and do all it can to support and equip families.

> It is time for the church to refuse to accept the current divorce rate and do all it can to support and equip families.

Families also are more fragmented than ever. Dads and moms are working more than forty hours a week and seeing less of their children. One study asked high school students what they wanted more of. While a minority wanted more money or a bigger house, the overwhelming majority wished for more time with their families.[7]

Jim Burns reminds us that families need help raising godly teens. He says,

> I'm truly thankful for the wonderful influence that
> youth ministries have – impacting and motivating the
> spiritual lives of our kids. Yet, far too many parents
> expect the church to instill the spiritual values their
> children need. Most parents have a difficult time pro-
> actively helping their children grow spiritually because
> they themselves didn't have adequate role models
> growing up.[8]

The same thing is said by another youth worker:

> In the past 50 years, even churched families have come
> to believe that dropping off kids is enough to guarantee
> the spiritual and character formation of their children.
> As a result, we have raised several underequipped gen-
> erations of Christian parents and grandparents who do
> not know how to equip their children in faith and char-
> acter. They can't teach them what they do not know.[9]

So where are families left to look for a model for Christian parenting? Where can they go for support in their marriage, encouragement in their relationships, and teaching advice for how to parent? The church must excel in instructing
and equipping moms and dads in all aspects of family life,
especially discipling their children. George Barna says, "In
situations where children became mature Christians, we usually found a symbiotic partnership between their parents and
their church." That's the biblical ideal. Many churches are

so busy running programs, filling slots, and maintaining the outward veneer there isn't enough time left for strengthening families. Churches must begin doing things differently, which is the second reason a strategy must be put in place to put parents back in the mix.

3) Limited influence

The third reason is common sense. Have you realized how quickly students move through our ministries? Our annual graduate breakfast amazes me year after year, as we have close to one hundred students in attendance for their last student ministry event. It's a blessing to me personally when I hear comments from the students encouraging and thanking our staff and me. They share their favorite memories, they promise to stay in touch, and a few tell us that they don't know how they will make it without us. What an ego boost. The strange thing, however, is that I never see these students at my house for Thanksgiving dinner or on Christmas morning. Where are they? Who are they with? It's simple. I believe the majority of them are with the most influential people in their lives: their parents and family.

One trait all students have in common is that they leave our student ministries. When you and I think of some students, that might bring us comfort, but 100 percent leave one way or another. Our influence is limited to a few years, and this fact must drive our ministry philosophy and actions. We may not be there when they struggle through college or discuss with them whom to marry. We may not be there when their first child is born or when most of adulthood's biggest moments and darkest days occur. We will likely be nowhere around, but their parents will be there. To influence these young people for the greatest amount of time, we must spend time equipping and pouring into those around them who will be there to give them godly advice long after they leave our ministries.

The average student spends approximately two hours at church per week. That is less than 2 percent of a teen's time.

Think about this. While they are under our influence, are we as youth workers teaching students to go to their parents for biblical wisdom and concerns, or do we enjoy the stream of young people coming to us for advice? It's great they can come to us, but when they go to college without ever being encouraged to go to their parents, who will they go ask? Their atheist biology teacher? Their nineteen-year-old roommate? It is even more alarming when studies show that college students drift away from the churches and ministers that they used to go to for advice.

If there is limited time, we must champion those who will be there for the long run. How many times have we said, "Great question, ask your dad or mom and come back and let me know what they said"? In the long run it is best to do everything we can to encourage the relationship with mom and dad since they have a much greater influence today and in the future than we will ever have. To ensure the advice they are giving their children is biblical, our church must teach and disciple parents.

4) Time with teens

Each week the students in our ministries have approximately 112 awake hours. How much of that time are our students under our care? The average student spends approximately two hours at church per week. That is less than 2 percent of a teen's time.

> To influence these young people for the greatest amount of time, we must spend time equipping and pouring into those around them who will be there to give them godly advice long after they leave our ministries.

Here's a visual illustration for you to share with your team or your teens' parents. Collect 112 ping-pong balls in a clear container for your next meeting (balloons or other types of balls may work as well). They should all be one color, except for two. Use the visual difference between the 110 and the two to demonstrate the imbalance we are describing. The vast majority of a student's time is spent away from student ministry. Imagine this proportion over a year of a student's life or the six to seven years in our ministries. Compare the time we spend trying to instill a biblical worldview to the time a teen spends being saturated by media.

One study concluded that teenagers spend more than twelve hours each week listening to the radio and another eight hours weekly listening to CDs and their iPods. According to a recent study from the University of Minnesota, listening to music is the primary way troubled teens say they cope with problems. (After music, they turn next to friends, drugs, and video games, the survey said. Talking with parents came near the bottom of the list. Tying for last place were teachers, clergy, and professional counselors.)[11]

We are competing with the worldview not only in the media, but also in the schools most of our teens attend:

> What about the influence of Sunday school and youth group programs? The Sunday school is another powerful influence for good, but it represents less than 1% of a child's time with perfect attendance in Sunday school. It's totally unrealistic for us as parents to assume that one hour of Sunday school, plus other church activities, can successfully compete with a 30-hour per week experience in a secular school.[12]

Early in my ministry I overestimated my influence. My distorted perspective caused me to dig in and protect the limited time that I felt was "mine." I had my time, and the parents had theirs. There was little or no crossover, and I failed to equip parents to make the most of the incredible amount of time that they have with their children. Three of the biggest mistakes I made as a young youth pastor were:

1. I assumed parents didn't want to disciple their children.
2. I believed parents didn't have as much influence on their teens as I did.
3. I enamored students to myself and did not champion the influencers who would walk throughout life with the students.

Unfortunately, many student pastors continue to be as shortsighted as I was, not thinking about how to influence the other 98 percent of our students' awake time. We squander one of our greatest resources when we fail to partner with parents. The truth is that most Christian parents want to see their children walking in the fullness of Christ, which is why they bring their children to you and me each week. We have the same goal, and it is time we join forces to accomplish it. For those parents who seem indifferent, we must humbly but confidently present the truth found in God's Word and urge them to be biblically obedient and do so in love. The limited time we have on a weekly basis with our students is yet another reason we need a strategy to bring parents back into the key part of the equation.

5) Adult volunteers

We work hard at Providence to ensure there are plenty of adult volunteers around our teens. We like to keep a one-to-eight ratio or better. That's one adult who is given the task to provide love, care, and a godly model for eight students. That's a big responsibility but a manageable one when we understand the volunteers are not the primary disciplers of students. In many churches, volunteers are assigned the task of shepherding and discipling eight or more teens. Remember, in many contexts these volunteers are in their twenties, have no kids of their own, are there for a short term, have limited time, and have no theological training. Yet, parents entrust these people with the spiritual well-being of their children and hope that by graduation a mature, spiritual young adult is produced. See a problem?

> The truth is that most Christian parents want to see their children walking in the fullness of Christ, which is why they bring their children to you and me each week. We have the same goal, and it is time we join forces to accomplish it.

Parents find it difficult in many churches to trust student ministry volunteers and sometimes rightly so. Many volunteers in the average student ministry are students who left the ministry when they graduated high school, but they weren't finished with fun student activities, so they became volunteers. Parents see their lack of maturity, biblical insight, and life experience. Yet, these are the ones in many churches left doing frontline teen ministry and counseling, providing support and opening the Word with them.

Wouldn't your student ministry be more productive by utilizing volunteers who are more mature, who parent teenagers, who've known the teens for years, and who greatly love the teens? These are the reasons God ordained parents, not church pastors or volunteers, to be the primary disciplers of teens. Swiss educator Johann Pestalozzi wrote, "The best way for a child to learn about God, is to know a real Christian. The best way for them to discover the power of prayers, is to live with parents who pray and truly walk with God."[13] Parents are primary.

Now that my three children are in my student ministry, I realize how impossible it is to believe that the church alone can disciple my children. Any parent making this assumption may be sorely disappointed, as studies now tell us. I do need the church's help, but the job is clearly Tina's and mine, and we accept that responsibility joyfully. Why would I, or any parent, want to give the highest calling for my life to someone else? If we seek to reassign the responsibility that God has given to us to someone else, we are simply rolling the dice with souls at stake.

In summary, there are numerous reasons a strategy must be implemented to ensure parents are championed in student ministries; we have looked at five. The Bible, today's research, and a good dose of common sense tell us we must identify ways to intentionally engage, equip, and edify parents. George Barna reveals that a majority of parents say they are struggling to create the type of spiritual family relationships that they desire. These parents admit the church is trying to provide them with useful information on parenting, but something is still missing.[14]

So, what is missing? What strategy can we put into place to ensure parents are the main part of the equation? We have been asked questions, like these from Chapter 4, about this exact subject:

- What role do parents play in the formation, direction, and execution of your student ministry?
- How are you motivating and equipping parents to develop the faith of teenagers in your ministry?
- What systems and structures are in place to support this model?

When people ask us questions like these, we respond by talking about "RTI," which stands for Resource, Train, and Involve. It is our three-step strategy to ensure parents are no longer sidelined in our ministry. We'll look at each part individually.

R: RESOURCE

Parents are resourced anytime they are given tools that allow them to guide, grow, train, or encourage their child's faith development. Most parents feel ill-prepared to create such resources. Studies show us that families are busier than ever, only having a little more than 30 minutes a week to spend in meaningful conversation with their children;[15] therefore, resources provide a great starting point for parents to disciple and mentor their children. Family devotions, prayer guides, and spiritual journals are examples of resources we offer our parents at different times in our ministry. Parents are able to take these resources fashioned for their use and adapt them to the needs of their family. As our church provides resources for our parents, they have expressed great appreciation for our partnership with them. One concerned person said it this way:

> Every argument I hear about this topic these days goes something like this... "How do we get parents involved in Youth ministry?" That's the wrong approach in my opinion. Since when is the 'Youth Ministry' the thing we need to get parents involved in? How about getting the family as a whole involved in the church. Parents don't like the idea of getting involved in the Youth ministry because they don't need 50 teenagers as best friends. However, offer them tools and encouragement in navigating the waters of raising an adolescent and they will come around.[16]

I had lunch one day with the father of one of our students who shared with me how Providence Student Ministries has changed him. He told me, "One of the greatest aspects of our ministry model isn't just that my children are growing but how God has grown me and my wife so that we would be greater spiritual models for our children to follow." Wow! That is what it is all about. Parents truly desire to be resourced when they realize the great role God has for them to play in their child's life.

T: TRAIN

A key component of seeing students becoming faithful followers of Christ is seen when their parents are engaged as the primary disciplers. Parents are equipped for this noble assignment in a variety of ways, including training in parenting, discipling, family, or marriage. We seek to prioritize the importance of family in all areas of church life. One of the core values at our church is the importance of family, meaning that family must be woven through the fabric of everything we do, including events such as parenting and marriage seminars, adult Bible studies, weekend retreats, and all of the student ministry programming.

Our student ministry started a monthly meeting for all parents called Parent Refuge, which meets on the same night as Refuge, our monthly student gathering. At these meetings, we equip parents through some type of training instead of simply reviewing the calendar and answering questions parents may have. We might bring in someone to talk about how to prepare a passage trip for them and their child, relational parenting, instructions and examples of how to journal to your children, family worship, or how to design a spiritual strategy for surviving the high school years. Once a year we hold a cookout with hamburgers and hot dogs just to get to know the new parents coming into our ministry. These meetings have become some of our best opportunities to equip parents and change families.

We've been encouraged as we've gone from a parent-meeting approach to a parent-equipping approach. An example of this is what happened one year during our Metamorphosis (our annual discipleship weekend) event for students. We typically kick this event off with a huge rally for our students, but several years ago we decided to ask parents to attend a separate kickoff rally just for them. My staff and I arranged fifty chairs with great anticipation, so we were overwhelmed when more than 250 parents attended this training session. One of our pastors encouraged parents to consider a relational view of parenting, which corresponded with the topic of the weekend. Our goal was very simple: let's get our parents and their children on the same page to encourage carryover at home. Ever since we adopted this way of thinking, we have been able to develop new ways like these to train parents.

> Parents are equipped for this noble assignment in a variety of ways, including training in parenting, discipling, family, or marriage.

I: INVOLVE

In 1996 more than two thousand professional student pastors were asked in a survey to reflect on the joys, struggles, likes, and dislikes of their profession. They were asked to complete sentences like "What I like most about youth ministry is..." "I wish I had more training in..." "It pleases me in youth ministry when..." "My biggest concern in youth ministry today is..." etc. Mark Lamport, professor and lead researcher at Huntington College, found that "the lack of parental cooperation with youth was a major concern."[17]

When many see the word *involve*, they think of the traditional ways we involve parents: chaperone a trip, teach a class, bring cookies, etc. While these are expressions of public ministry, a greater level of involvement which we desire from our parents is their personal ministry at home. Personal ministry refers to a level of involvement that is harder to see: parents embracing their role as primary disciplers within their family. We would like parents worshiping as a family at home rather than chaperoning a ski trip because we think that involvement produces greater results. We would rather see a mom faithfully praying for her son than bringing a casserole to his Bible study. We would like to see a dad writing in his daughter's transition journal rather than standing along the back wall during a student rally. The most important involvement from parents is when they embrace the biblical assignment to become spiritual leaders to their families.

Practical ways in which parents in our ministry are doing this include:

- family worship time
- family mission trips
- journaling to their children
- passage and journey transition events
- praying daily for and with their spouses and children

God ordained parents to be the primary disciplers because it allows children to have daily influence, rather than only two hours a week of outside influence. Parents become involved in personal ministry when they serve as daily mentors to their children. The greatest sense of satisfaction for my staff and me is when parents embrace their personal ministry and responsibility to disciple their children in their homes.

The second way parents are involved is through their public ministry—the traditional ways we can all see at church. At our church, we want to shatter the widely accepted concept by some parents that their job is to just bring their children to us, so we place parents in public roles in several ways. First we want parents to be visible; we want our parents to always feel welcome to attend student ministry events whenever possible. Also, our first appeal for workers is always made to our parents. As we have sought to involve parents in every area of our ministry, the percentage of parents serving continues to rise. We work hard to find ways for parents to engage in public ministry. Some of these ways include opening their homes to discipleship groups, teaching Sunday morning classes, serving as small group counselors at camp, leading hospitality teams, forming prayer teams, hosting socials, helping with administrative duties, directing ministry events, driving students on trips, attending weekly ministry events, participating in events that allow them to make spiritual markers and memories with their children, etc.

One final way we seek to engage parents in the formation, direction, and execution of our ministry to students and their parents is with our Parent Leadership Team (PLT). We hope we are going a step further in involving our parents, by actually allowing them to help guide and shape our ministry to their children. If we are serious about partnering with parents, it is our conviction that we must allow them to influence us, not just the other way around. It is tragic that some student pastors claim a ministry partnership with parents but fail to gain the great depth of insight that parents undeniably offer. More details about our PLT will be covered in Chapter 6.

> If we are serious about partnering with parents, it is our conviction that we must allow them to influence us, not just the other way around.

TRUE PARTNERSHIP

Can you honestly think of a tougher job in the world than parenting? Believe it or not our parents really do want to do a good job. They are very concerned for their child's spiritual condition but many times feel paralyzed by self-doubt, personal inadequacies, and the fear of the unknown. Imagine how encouraged parents would be by our efforts to resource them in creative ways and by our desire to equip them for their eternal work of spiritual formation. Recently a student pastor mentioned that his senior pastor wanted him to have a parent team help shape and sharpen their student ministry. The student pastor told him, "No way; why would I seek their help when *they* do not even know where *I* am heading and where *I* am taking this ministry?" Doesn't sound like much of a partnership, does it? It's hypocritical to want parents to move towards us if we aren't willing to move towards them. Do we really desire a true partnership with our parents? Do we value their contribution, and do we give them opportunities to tell us how we can help them do their jobs better? I hope we can begin doing so.

Think about how supportive parents could become if we were to invite them to roll up their sleeves and engage in ministry with us. Imagine what your ministry might become if parents realized that we truly valued their contributions and that everything we do is an effort to lock arms with them. At every student ministry event at our church we seek, resource, train, or involve parents. Every event. With everything we

■ reTHiNK

plan my staff knows this question is coming from me: "How can we involve parents in this process?"

Because we know God has a great dream and purpose for all of our students, we will endeavor to engage parents in every way as they possess an incredibly powerful, God-given influence in their children's lives. Mike DeVries says it right:

The role of the church has remained the same, and our goal as youth workers is to stand alongside parents in helping them pass on the faith to their children. Youth ministry of the future must not be about adding more programming to help our students meet Jesus better. We need to be more holistic in our approach, not only in spiritual formation issues, but also in the factors and people that are brought in to influence the lives of students. It'll take more than just a youth group meeting to see students' experiences of God enriched. We must bring parents back into the circumstances and situations of their children and re-introduce parents into the spiritual formation equation. Parents are too valuable to leave out.[18]

> Youth ministry of the future must not be about adding more programming to help our students meet Jesus better.

NOTES:

1 Bruce Wilkinson, *The Prayer of Jabez* (Sisters, OR: Multnomah Publishers, 2000) p.32.

2 Steve Farrar, *King Me: What Every Son Wants and Needs from His Father*. (Chicago: Moody Publishers, 2005) pp.20-21.

3 Dr. Richard Land, *For Faith and Family* (Nashville: Broadman & Holman Publishers, 2002) p.67.

4 Ibid., pp.16-17.

5 Ibid., p.67.

6 *Marriage in America: A Report to the Nation* (New York: Institute for American Values, 1995), p.8.

7 *The State Of Our Nation's Youth: 2005-2006* (Alexandria, VA: Horatio Alger Association, 2006) p.32, downloaded from horatioalger.org.

8 Jim Burns, taken from www.homeword.com/Articles/ArticleDetail. aspx?iArticleId=279.

9 Judy Gregory, taken from www.judygregory.blogspot.com/2007/05/orange-part-2-partnering-with-parents.html.

10 George Barna, taken from www.sundaysoftware.com/stats.htm.

11 Stat taken from www.csrnet.org/csrnet/articles/perilous-times.html.

12 From "Five Reasons for Christian Education," taken from www.amana. co.nz/5reasons/influence.html.

13 Johann Pestalozzi, taken from www.guideyourchildren.com.

14 George Barna, *Ministering to the Family: The Foundation of a Spiritual Revolution*. A video seminar (Ventura, CA: Regal Books. 1998).

15 American Family Research Council, "Parents Fight 'Time Famine' as Economic Pressures Increase," 1990.

16 Taken from a post on www.timschmoyer.com/2007/06/25/two-approaches-to-youth-ministry.

17 Merton Strommen and Richard Hardel, *Passing on the Faith* (Winona, MI: Saint Mary's Press, 2000), p.198.

18 Mike DeVries. "Worshipping at the Altar of Me: The Role of Parents in Kids' Spiritual Formation" taken from www.youthspecialties.com/articles/topics/family/altar.php.

reDiscover:

Spiritual

Formation

You may have heard of Vanuatu, an island in the South Pacific recently featured on the television show *Survivor*. A couple of hundred years ago, the island was called the New Hebrides and was filled with a people group of savage islanders known for cannibalism. The first missionaries to the island were killed, cooked, and eaten, and few people dared to visit the island. John Paton was born in the 1820s in Scotland and felt a strong calling to go to Vanuatu. Many friends and family discouraged his going; regardless, he moved there and ministered for years. Within the first months of arriving in Vanuatu, John's wife and son became ill and died. Much of his early work was completed while living in daily fear that he might become the savages' next meal. He slept with his clothes on so he could run at a moment's notice, and more than once he had a spear pointed at him. He claimed the Lord restrained their hands from killing him. He wrote:

> I realized that I was immortal till my Master's work with me was done. The assurance came to me, as if a voice out of Heaven had spoken, that not a musket would be fired to wound us, not a club prevail to strike us, not a spear leave the hand in which it was held vibrating to be thrown, not an arrow leave the bow, or a killing stone the fingers, without the permission of Jesus Christ, whose is all power in Heaven and on Earth. He rules all Nature, animate and inanimate, and restrains even the Savage of the South Seas.[1]

The lasting impact of John Paton on Vanuatu continues today. *Operation World* states that 85 percent of the population of the island identify themselves as Christian because of Paton's ministry.[2] While he was there he translated the New Testament into the local language, and this translation is still in use today. Paton was used by God to change the island from being known for cannibalism to being known as Christian.

Paton is a hero of the faith, and his legacy continues today. However, the story doesn't end there, nor did it start there. You should get to know two other heroes—his student ministers. The ones who discipled him and gave him the model to follow have stories just as amazing and even more challenging. Here is what Paton wrote about his student ministers:

Thither (in the closet) daily, and oftentimes a day, generally after each meal, we saw our father retire, and "shut the door"; and we children got to understand by a sort of spiritual instinct (for the thing was too sacred to be talked about) that prayers were being poured out there for us, as of old by the High Priest within the veil of the Most Holy Place. We occasionally heard the pathetic echoes of a trembling voice pleading as if for life, and we learned to slip out and in past that door on tiptoe, not to disturb that holy colloquy. The outside world might not know, but we knew, whence came that happy light as of a new-born smile that always was dawning on my father's face: it was a reflection from the Divine Presence, in the consciousness of which he lived... Though everything else in religion were by some unthinkable catastrophe to be swept out of my memory, or blotted from my understanding, my soul would wander back to those early scenes, and shut itself up once again in that Sanctuary Closet, and, hearing still the echoes of those cries to God, would hurl back all doubt with the victorious appeal, "He walked with God, why may not I?"[3]

John's parents, James and Janet Paton, were the student ministers in his life, and their faith changed his life forever. He wrote about the power of his father's prayers and how they changed one woman's life. He wrote about an "immoral" woman who lived near them and recorded,

> [The only thing that] kept her from despair and from the Hell of the suicide, was when in the dark winter nights she crept close up underneath my father's window, and heard him pleading in Family Worship that God would convert "the sinner from the error of wicked ways, and polish him as a jewel for the Redeemer's crown." She said this, "I felt that I was a burden on that good man's heart, and I knew that God would not disappoint him. That thought kept me out of hell and at last led me to the only Saviour."[4]

John's father also taught his children the importance of church, which included a four-mile walk that he made weekly with his family in tow. The walk to church was a time John and his ten other siblings looked forward to. John wrote that his dad only missed church three times—once for a terrible ice storm, once for a snowstorm, and once for a cholera outbreak when the church leadership wrote their family a letter that John mentioned:

> The farmers and villagers, suspecting that no cholera would make my father stay at home on a Sabbath, sent

a deputation to my mother on the Saturday evening,
and urged her to restrain his devotions for once![5]

The road to the mission field wasn't easy for John. People were aware (and wanted to make sure John was keenly aware) of the dangers of this island of savages and cannibals. A concerned acquaintance tried to talk sense into John and realized the depth of his conviction when he said, "I confess to you that if I can but live and die serving and honoring the Lord Jesus, it will make no difference to me whether I am eaten by Cannibals or by worms."[6] When he became overwhelmed with the number of people trying to discourage him from going to Vanuatu, his parents wrote him a letter saying,

Heretofore we feared to bias you, but now we must tell you why we praise God for the decision to which you have been led. Your father's heart was set up being a Minister, but other claims forced him to give it up. When you were given to them, your father and mother laid you upon the altar, their first-born, to be consecrated, if God saw fit, as a Missionary of the Cross; and it has been their constant prayer that you might be prepared, qualified, and led to this very decision; and we pray with all our heart that the Lord may accept your offering, long spare you, and give you many souls from the Heathen World for your hire.[7]

John then confidently wrote, "From that moment, every doubt as to my path of duty forever vanished."[8] It was God using his parents' influence that made John a hero of the faith.

John Paton's story reminds us that parents have the greatest influence for Christ. Not the church leadership. Not school teachers. Not student pastors. God has given parents a position of influence that cannot be equaled. David Wells rightly calls the family "the conduit of values from one generation to the next."[9]

When we come to a full understanding of the role that God desires for parents to play, the question isn't so much "How can we involve parents?" but rather "How could we not involve them?" When I consider the impact of a person like John Paton as opposed to the current, accepted goal of just hoping our students are still claiming faith after college graduation—I like the former. For those who might say we don't have parents today like James and Janet Paton, I encourage you to consider Ephesians 4:11-13:

> It was he who gave some to be apostles, some to be prophets, some to be evangelists, and some to be pastors and teachers, to prepare God's people for works of service, so that the body of Christ may be built up until we all reach unity in the faith and in the knowledge of the Son of God and become mature, attaining to the whole measure of the fullness of Christ.

Few parents know how to rear their children into the fullness of Christ; this is where we come in. Our biblically given job is preparing these parents to disciple their children. As we previously stated, this chapter will continue to answer some commonly asked questions. We will focus on two questions I put under the category of spiritual formation — that is, how we restore parents' understanding of their role as the primary shapers of their children's spiritual lives. These questions came from the same e-mails mentioned in Chapter 4:

- What role do parents play in the formation, direction, and execution of your student ministry?
- How do you involve the church body in the spiritual formation of students in your ministry?

In answering these questions we will see several teams and strategies we have put in place to put parents back in the driver's seat of their child's spiritual formation. The first team we'll cover is the Parent Leadership Team (PLT).

PARENT LEADERSHIP TEAM

Our student ministry is excited that God has granted us the opportunity to partner with the primary disciplers of our students. This partnership is based on resourcing, training, and involving parents in the overall formation, direction, and execution of our student ministry. The primary way we involve parents at this directional level is through our PLT. There really isn't anything we do as a ministry that doesn't have the thumbprint of the PLT on it. My staff is blessed to work with such a wonderful, fun team that volunteers their time to invest faithfully in our combined efforts to strengthen families and develop students. There are five convictions that lead us to involve parents in this foundational way:

1. We believe a true partnership with parents must tap into the richness of life experiences and wisdom that has been gained from those who have raised teens.

2. We believe a ministry that has been shaped by parents of teens will look significantly different than a ministry shaped exclusively by young adults who haven't been blessed with the joys, frustrations, and experiences of having teenagers.

3. We believe a much greater level of confidence, trust, and grace is established with all parents in our ministry when they know their peers are involved in the planning, execution, and evaluation of every ministry effort.

4. We believe a complete team must give greater consideration to all families represented in our church body, including single parent homes, foster care, divorced or separated, public school, home school, private school families, etc.

5. We believe stronger relationships are established between parents and church leadership when they pray, dream, struggle, listen, and share together.

PLT: LEADING THE WAY

The guiding principles of Ephesians 4 and the RTI (Resource, Train, Involve) strategy mandate that we educate and equip parents; however, a partnership is not just a one-sided relationship. If they are our partners, we cannot do all the talking and them do all the listening. Doesn't sound like a partnership to me. The PLT is our turn to listen, to be the ones asking the questions instead of always coming up with the answers.

There are about twelve people on our PLT, including staff members and married and single adults who currently have or previously had children in our ministry. We typically meet five or six times a year, and I meet with individual group members as needed. During our meetings, we pray, discuss issues, share concerns, evaluate the ministry, and dream together as well as comfort and support one another. It is humbling to see how each member has been faithful to invest and pour themselves into my team, my family, and myself. I will always remember how this group of friends ministered to us through the toughest ministry situation I have ever experienced. I am convinced that without the prayers and partnership of this group, our ministry to students, parents, and families would only be a fraction of what it is today.

> It is humbling to see how each member has been faithful to invest and pour themselves into my team, my family, and myself.

PARENT LEADERSHIP TEAM
JOB DESCRIPTION

PLT Purpose

Provide wisdom, information, encouragement, and perspective to the Student Ministry Leadership Team concerning every aspect of Providence Student Ministries.

One-Word Summary

Advise

Synonyms

Recommend, Suggest, Counsel, Caution, Warn, Admonish, Give Perspective

Expectations

PLT is a Parent-Led Ministry

PLT Focus

1. Prayer for Student Ministries leadership
2. Observation of Student Ministries
3. Attendance of ministry events
4. Advocating of ministry direction and staff

Ministry Focus

1. Create ways to resource, train, and involve parents
2. Encourage adult workers
3. Assist with parent meetings

Lead Parent

This person will be selected by PLT members at year-end meeting to serve during the upcoming year. The Lead Parent's role includes:

1. Set meeting schedule and agenda
2. Advise team of all scheduled meetings
3. Conduct PLT meetings
4. Invite new members to serve as needed

PLT Rotation

PLT members each serve a two-year term with two new couples rotating on each year.

This may not seem like an earth-shaking concept, and you're right. I've worked with parent teams in other churches, but the team described above functions on a different level. The key element for this team came when they understood a biblical framework for student ministry and when they took ownership of how we ministered to parents.

The process began when we asked two important gut-check questions:

1. Do I truly value the contribution of others over my own agenda?

2. What role do I believe parents should play in a ministry to their children?

Our answers make a team like the PLT indispensable, and we have been sharpened and deepened ever since.

A few years ago I received a phone call from a student pastor concerning our PLT. His questions began the usual way: "How many parents? What are their roles? When do they rotate off? Is it a committee or an advisory team?" At the end of our conversation, he finally asked the big question—"What would I do if I wanted to do something, and all the parents in the room felt God wanted to go a different direction?" I call this the lone-wolf mentality. I shared with him that this had never happened with our PLT. However, I respect the people I have on my team so much that if I were outnumbered to that extent, I would realize my perspective was wrong. I would then yield to what the PLT is all about; I'd listen to the perspective of our parents.

The truth is that any ministry we lead is not really our ministry. This is an incredibly freeing realization. First, the ministry is God's, meaning you and I have the tremendous privilege to minister to those God created and loves, namely teens and their parents. Second, parents should be the primary ministers to their teens, and the practical ministry should be led by godly, church-centered parents. If we understand their vital role in student ministry, then they must have a venue to talk while we listen to them. I'm not saying that you should act upon every suggestion they make, but our ministries would be sharpened tremendously when we ask parents, "How can we better partner with you as we both seek to spiritually disciple your children?"

> The truth is that any ministry we lead is not really our ministry. This is an incredibly freeing realization.

DISCOVERY TEAM

Another way we involve parents in the formation and execution of our ministry is through the Discovery Team. We recently asked six couples, a single mom, two students, and a few youth workers to join us in a four-month discovery process. The two questions we considered were:

1. What would a student ministry built only on biblical principles look like?
2. How can we better partner with parents as they seek to become disciplers of their children?

I gave them three nonnegotiable parameters to guide our conversations:

1. Pray, pray, pray. I wanted them to know that the outcome of our meetings would greatly impact families and students. We needed God to provide a depth of insight that none of us possess on our own.
2. Dig into God's Word. I wasn't interested in hearing about personal agendas (which we all have—me included) or about the latest fad or about what the church down the street was doing. Our goal was to discover real ways our ministry could better align with a biblical framework.
3. Build an open, trusting environment. I wanted the group to know that we could share and talk about the sacred cows and the untouchables. This was a place to question and discover together.

Our group met four times, and members were very open and honest, which was beneficial to my staff and me. Meetings typically lasted two to three hours as we prayed together, challenged one another spiritually, and dreamed together of what "could be."

An example of how our ministry was sharpened through the Discovery Team's process can be seen below. We encouraged team members to offer contributions and ideas. One of our parents asked if he could share an idea he felt the Lord had led him to, and it was a bit outside the box. The following represents how this parent suggested that Refinery, our discipleship ministry for teens, could be strengthened. (Refinery is a collection of small groups that meet in homes and are facilitated by two volunteers. They are age-graded, are divided by gender, and meet all but one Wednesday night a month.)

ONE PARENT'S PERSPECTIVE

Preface: The Discovery Team has requested that team members submit creative ideas that incorporate initiatives and priorities that have surfaced in our Discovery Team sessions.

The Discovery Team has prayerfully comprised a list of important components of an ideal youth ministry. The top six are as follows:

1 God's Word/Biblically based
2 Parent Partnership
3 Discipleship
4 Fellowship
5 Glorifying God
6 Accountability

The Problem: While Refinery is a great ministry, it can always be strengthened. Below are a couple of observations that I have heard in the Discovery Team meetings, and from discussions with other parents, Refinery leaders, students, etc.

- Discipleship is ultimately the job of the parent. Refinery was not meant to replace that responsibility. But, Refinery leaders have a broad directive, which can place undue burden towards thinking they have that responsibility.
- It is very difficult to keep writing devotions for 36 or 52 weeks of the year and coordinating Refinery group discussion time in concert with such devotions.
- The parents are rarely aware of what is discussed in Refinery and are not given a specific challenge to partner with this ministry.
- Discipleship is not happening in those groups as intended, and it probably should not as, again, it is the parents' responsibility.
- Fellowship is segregated as the gender groups of each grade are divided. This has some small group benefits, but it also lends itself toward solidifying cliques and bending the students toward not reaching out to other cliques. Unity of the class always suffers.
- Further, accountability is not in concert with the parents but directed without guidance from the parents.
- We are producing students who rarely read the Bible

because the focus has been on "curriculum." Need more be said on that one?

A Potential Solution: The solution below is structured in the order of the above "Top 6" Important Components.

1. Make Refinery totally biblically based. In other words, have it based solely on reading and discussing God's Word. Don't bother with having customized devotions. Let their devotions be simply reading the Bible. We have had some experience with this. We have learned that a one-year plan is hard to do for a student with a narrow attention span. But, a seven-year Bible-reading plan would be much easier on several levels. This also can serve as a vehicle to give students a framework for reading the entire Bible throughout their seven years in student ministry. The devotions can simply be a daily assignment of Bible reading for five days of the week in concert with a seven-year plan for reading the entire Bible. As part of their devotions, they can simply answer the three questions: 1) What is the writer saying? 2) What one question do I have? 3) How can I apply this to my life? This eliminates the need to "pull rabbits out of hats" in writing seven years' worth of devotions for every week of the year. It would just be an expected part of participation with Refinery. It will allow the "Refining" to happen more directly from

God's Word rather than just the thoughts of well-written devotionals.

2. Partner with the parents. Publish this Bible reading/devotional plan to the parents and on the Students page of the church website where every parent can easily access it every day. Invite every parent to challenge his or her student to take this plan seriously. Invite parents to use this plan as part of their family devotions. Push this responsibility to the parents as part of their discipleship of the students. No, not every parent will take advantage of this, but we are not looking for perfection. We are looking for partnering. The parents who do take it seriously will appreciate it and see it as a wonderful partnering opportunity. Further, the devotional plan of the three simple questions mentioned above is simple for any parent to follow. If a parent chooses not to take advantage of the opportunity, that is his/her decision, and everyone would be okay with that.

3. Discipleship. This recognizes the role of discipleship on the part of the parents and provides a vehicle to urge it in that direction. Again, not all parents will take part in this. But for those that do, they will have a simple opportunity to disciple their children over a seven-year term with the help of a younger partner (Refinery leader) who will support them in that endeavor. The Refinery leader becomes a facilitator and supporter of the parent in this endeavor, not the main discipler. Their role will be to answer questions once a week and hold them accountable to their parents.

4. Fellowship. There is a compromise between small group accountability and large group fellowship. If you have ALL of one gender meet at the same house, you can foster fellowship with the entire grade and not just a pre-designed clique. Then at the end of every Refinery meeting, you can break up into pre-designed smaller prayer groups. These groups would be the same throughout the entire year. You could still assign enough Refinery leaders to one house that you need to cover all of the small prayer groups. But, this would allow for small group accountability and prayer, while not sacrificing fellowship across a class grade. It is important to note that while there are many good reasons for splitting up into small groups, a prominent reason was small group discipleship. What we have learned is that it doesn't work because, again, that is the primary responsibility of the parents.

5. Glorifying God. There is no question that doing this will glorify God. What could be more important than a targeted emphasis on saturating our youth with His Word? Further, an initiative toward encouraging the parents in partnership toward more effective discipleship will reap wonderful fruit for many of our families.

This will be more glorifying to God than the present structure.

6. Accountability. This also has not worked for several reasons. But, if accountability is targeted to be in support of parents, rather than in addition to the parents, that can be easier to bite off and be more effective. We should target the accountability toward the reading of God's Word in concert with the parents. If a student wants to take that further, they are always welcome to be held accountable in other ways if they choose to be. Accountability, however, does not need to be sold in a hard fashion. A Refinery leader looking you in the eye every week and asking you what God taught you through the reading of His Word for that week and/or discussing it with your parents that week will be very enlightening.

Okay, that is my creative idea. Please don't throw large blunt objects at me.

–A Partnering Parent

These ideas were developed, prayed over, and presented to us by a parent. My intent in sharing the document is to provide an example of how parents can help shape your ministry to their children. Student pastors may see ideas like these as a challenge to their power, which is unfortunate. What is even more regrettable is that the majority of student pastors will never see ideas like these because there is no forum where parents are welcomed to share them. These thoughts are incredible, especially the ones that encourage parents to read the Bible along with their teens. We have integrated most of these ideas into our ministry, which has been strengthened as a result. We are better because parents are seen as true partners and are welcome to sharpen us and add incredible value to our combined ministry to their children.

CHURCH-WIDE EFFORTS

The second question we are frequently asked is, "How do you involve the church body in the spiritual formation of students in your ministry?" Good question.

I was surprised one day to receive a phone call from two parents who are members of a large Protestant church in our area. They had heard about how we are doing ministry and wanted to meet with me to discuss their concerns about the increasing number of students who drop out of church life after their confirmation. I shared with them the problems we all face with the current model of student ministry, our need to discover a biblical framework, and that God has called parents to be the primary spiritual disciplers of their children. While they quickly agreed they needed help from their church leadership, they weren't sure if they could ask for the help. They believed their church was too busy with the many programs already in place. Equipping parents on top of the other programs they are doing may be too much.

Is the church too busy? If so, what is it busy doing?

Many churches today view busyness as the norm, and it is embraced by its flummoxed leadership as the way we do church today. Pastors feel there is a pervasive apathy among its membership, and they often say, "Christianity for much of our congregation is only 'coming to church.'" Maybe church members think this way because it is what we have taught them. Maybe our members think this way because we have come to measure success in terms of growing church attendance, constructing new church buildings, and maintaining a busy church calendar. Dare I suggest that how we measure success may not be as important as how we define success? Look around—when we see children scarred by divorce, parents who have nowhere to turn for help, prevailing sin in open display, an unreached world that has never heard the good news of Christ, families ripped apart by addictions and violence, teens in open rebellion—can we honestly say we're too busy "ministering"? Those we are supposed to equip are being trampled in the rat race of church busyness, and it is time for us to slow down and go after those who have been left on the sidelines.

It is incredible to me that we even have to point out that one of the church's priorities should be to equip parents. We must move beyond the quick-fix parenting seminars that give

> Dare I suggest that how we measure success may not be as important as how we define success?

parents five easy ways to stop their teenagers' back-talking and instead instruct parents how they might teach the Word at home, lead their child to Christ, and use daily problems to point their children toward God. We no longer can take our cues from the self-help aisle at the bookstore or the daytime talk shows; we must get in the trenches with families to help them discover how to become the type of parents depicted in Deuteronomy 6.

We believe that the church as a whole can assist with a student's spiritual formation and faith development.

When was the last time you heard a church say to its families, "God intends for you to disciple your children, and we are going to show you how to do it"? What about, "Dads, you must be the spiritual shepherd of your home, and we will teach you how to begin praying for your family"? Have you heard, "Moms, you play a critical role in the spiritual formation of your children; because of this we want to help you become intentional with this God-given assignment"? Our church is striving to be that kind of church.

The emphasis that Providence places on glorifying God above all else has allowed me to look beyond the significance of event attendance to focus on the significance of students' lives being built for kingdom use and equipped to defend their faith. It has allowed the church, its ministries, and its pastors freedom to partner with parents in the spiritual formation of our students. We believe that the church as a whole can assist with a student's spiritual formation and faith development in four ways:

1. Our students' faith development is shaped by our church's overall teaching and preaching ministry.
2. Our students' faith development is shaped by our efforts to engage our pastors and parents in student ministry events as often as possible. Some of these efforts include:

- Recruiting pastors to speak at youth camp, Metamorphosis, and other events
- Asking pastors to speak at monthly student gatherings
- Inviting pastors to visit Refinery small groups on Wednesday night and classes on Sunday morning
- Offering parents some of the same classes as their students
- Giving parents training during some student ministry events
- Encouraging parents to attend parent/student events (father/son hunting, mother/daughter purity conferences, etc.)

3. Our students' faith development is shaped by our church through its core values.

- We seek to strengthen families through an integrated ministry approach.
- We seek to see all ministries working together, locking

arms in a streamlined ministry approach. We do not continue to add programs upon programs.

- We seek a decentralized ministry mind-set that doesn't overemphasize "How many are at church?"

4. Our students' faith development is shaped by a principle-driven student ministry approach that views parents as indispensable ministry partners.

- Parents are viewed as primary disciplers.
- Student ministry is viewed as a secondary developer.

As you can see, we receive a lot of support from pastors and parents in how we do student ministry, but it doesn't stop there. Other ministries also understand they must do all they can to support families. It is not a "your job" mentality; it is everyone's job to equip families, and other ministries in our church understand that. Some of the things other ministries are doing to champion families include:

- Senior Pastor - David Horner has given us vision, articles, conferences, sermons, staff exhortation, and a personal model to follow. He champions this framework for ministry reminding us, "Churches cannot provide what families neglect."[10] His vision, which is driven by biblical principles, encourages all ministry leaders to resource, train, and involve parents in all aspects of our endeavors.
- Education Ministry - Leon Tucker, our discipleship pastor, has helped with everything from vision to execution and has helped these ideas cross over to different edu-

cation ministries. He also leads parent training sessions to help our parents understand relational parenting.

- Children's Ministry - Students are encouraged to serve with their parents at Super Summer Adventure (Vacation Bible School). The ministry also has its own version of the PLT called the "Two Cents" Parent Input Group and also hosts periodic parent forums. It offers a parent/child Sunday School option, as well as several parent/child fun nights.

- Women's Ministry - This ministry has been an indispensable partner with Student Ministries. We take the lead sometimes, and at other times they lead, but regardless of who leads, moms and daughters are impacted every time we work together. Moms are encouraged to bring their teens to summer Bible studies, fellowships, and Legacy of Love workshops. The Women's Ministry helped us plan a Modesty Conference for daughters and their moms. The event was greatly strengthened by the vision and partnership with the Women's Ministry.

- Men's Ministry - Almost every Men's Ministry event is open to dads and their sons/daughters. These events include: Men's Monday Night Bible Study, Summer Fly Fishing Trip to Wyoming, Fall Manly Event, Fall Salt Water Fishing Trip, Fall Bike Trip, Sporting Clay Shoot twice a year, Fall Boar Hunt, Winter Duck Hunt, Men's Ski Day, Kayaking/Fishing/Camping weekend, and other events and retreats.

- Missions - While you may think that it would be difficult for the Missions Ministry to find ways to support parents, the ministry leadership encourages families to go on family mission trips by offering trips that young people can attend with their parents and other adults.
- Community Ministries - Not long ago this ministry asked Student Ministries to help with some local needs. The exciting part was they asked for dads and sons to work together. Instead of simply asking our ministry to send a dozen high school boys, they recognized value in asking sons to work with their dads. What a great idea, and it was one we didn't initiate because another ministry had already adopted a similar mind-set.

Everyone in our church has some responsibility to come alongside parents, and these ideas are only a fraction of the strategic ministry efforts occurring at Providence. When churches leave behind a siloed approach to ministry and make every effort to partner with parents, families are impacted and young peoples' lives are changed. This really is the goal of a biblical student ministry approach and the essence of this book: to see parents in charge of the spiritual formation of their children and the lives of young people transformed. When the entire church resources, trains, and involves parents, we equip parents with the tools to bring up spiritual heroes. Maybe then we'll see transformed families. Maybe we'll see a generation of teens ready to impact the world for Christ. Maybe we'll see more John Patons in the world.

We'll end just where we began this chapter, looking at the incredible family of John Paton. He learned about Christ from the words of his father and mother. He saw it modeled in family worship. He heard it in the prayers of his dad. He wrote:

> When, on his knees and all of us kneeling around him in Family Worship, he poured out his whole soul with tears for the conversion of the Heathen World to the service of Jesus, and for every personal and domestic need, we all felt as if in the presence of the living Savior, and learned to know and love Him as Our Divine Friend.[11]

The scene ends with John standing on the dock ready to leave for a land of cannibals and spiritual darkness:

> I watched through blinding tears, till his form faded from my gaze, and then, hastening on my way, vowed deeply and oft, by the help of God, to live and act so as never to grieve or dishonor such a father and mother as He had given me.[12]

May we see this kind of spiritual formation between parent and teen in our ministries today.

NOTES:

1 John Paton, *An Autobiography: Missionary to the New Hebrides/Vanuatu* (Banner of Truth Trust, 2002) p.207.

2 Patrick Johnstone, *Operation World* (STL Books and WEC Publications, 1978) p.442.

3 Paton, An Autobiography, p.8.

4 Ibid.

5 Ibid., p.15.

6 Ibid., p.56.

7 Ibid., p.57.

8 Ibid., p.57.

9 Quote taken from a seminary lecture which can be found at www.covenantseminary.edu/resource/ResultDetail.asp.

10 David Horner, *Firmly Rooted, Faithfully Growing Principle-Based Ministry in the Church.* (2001) p.58.

11 Paton, p.21.

12 Ibid., pp.25-26.

reGrouP:

Facing and Overcoming Obstacles

Have you ever been to a conference or read a book and realized the further you went, the more overwhelmed you've become? All the information, all the ideal results, all the perfect stories seem great, but they don't seem to fit your reality. I certainly hope this book's contents haven't overwhelmed you. My intent is to encourage you to rethink what our ministries can become. Like you, I am a student pastor day in and day out, and my world isn't any more perfect than yours. I've got problems, you've got problems, and all God's children have problems. Many of the problems I faced were self-inflicted, and I'm afraid I'm not finished learning from the mistakes I make.

At my first church, Northlake, I made a mistake even bigger than punching Ricky. It's true. The biggest mistake, by far, I made at Northlake was my ongoing effort to effect lasting change in students' lives by being a friend to the students and not being a leader. I was fresh out of college, and I honestly thought the cool factor I brought to the table was a plus. Wow, what a bumpy experience that caused for everyone. If I could go back and do this one over, I would place greater value on being respected than being liked. I never earned the respect of parents because half the time they thought I was one of the students based on the way I acted.

My second church was First Lenoir City. My tenure there was the shortest of my churches, and it's not hard to see why. Even worse than not having any balance in my life was never allowing people close enough to protect me. I loved seeing all those plates spinning. The more plates I had going meant more people being reached, the more the church was growing, and the better student pastor I thought I was becoming. Even if my life, my marriage, and my ministry might derail. I was on the fast track to burnout and didn't even know it. On Mondays, I drove four hours to attend seminary classes (which started at noon and ended at 10:00 p.m.), then I drove four hours back home. I also took several weeklong intensive classes in New Orleans. I was a full-time student pastor with well over a hundred students, and I had a fairly new marriage with a baby daughter and another baby on the way. I wore my busyness like a badge of honor, thinking a frantic schedule equaled faithful service to God. The important thing to me was keeping everyone impressed, so I kept spinning those plates. Encourage parents? Are you kidding? How could I? I was busy enough doing other things "for God."

At my next church, Roebuck Park, I bought into the lie of "build it and they will come." *Bigger* and *better* were our two favorite words. I didn't want the world to offer a better "product" than the church, so we pulled out all the stops and spared no expense. I willingly jumped on the treadmill of "more, more, more." The leadership asked us to produce the numbers, and boy did we produce. Everyone waited to see which rabbit I would pull out of the hat next. The applause grew louder as the crowds grew, and it distracted me from asking the tough questions. We relied on the show to attract students, and I will have to ashamedly admit that event attendance became our gauge of success. If I could go back, I would seek to build disciples over building crowds. I would seek the applause of heaven over the applause of men and seek a biblical model that produces lasting fruit.

If I could start over at Providence, I would strive to be a better listener. I remember so many conversations with parents who came to me and genuinely wanted to help, but I tried to assure them that I had everything together. I would think, "I've been to seminary," or "I have years of experience," or "I've got all the bases covered." Three moms met with me once about a concern they had about our discipleship ministry. They felt it was difficult for our young ladies to focus on being discipled when the girls were being distracted by boys in their group. I assumed these moms were overprotective and overreacting. I thought to myself, "If I don't put the boys and girls together, no one would be discipled because no one would attend!" I wondered why these moms couldn't see that. The fact is they were right; I was wrong, completely wrong. Once we tried their suggestion of separating boys and girls, not only did we have better discipleship in the groups, but our attendance went through the roof.

> People have said that when you stop changing, you are dead. I understand what they mean.
>
> Ministry isn't static.
>
> The culture changes.
>
> Teens are changing.

More students were experiencing greater discipleship. I had valued "my way" over the contribution of others with whom I claimed to be partnering. How many other ideas to improve our ministry have I missed because I wasn't a good listener?

I have been asked many times, "How did you transition into this framework for ministry?" I can't help but smile and respond that I am still in transition. I'm still learning, growing, and changing. People have said that when you stop changing, you are dead. I understand what they mean. Ministry isn't static. The culture changes. Teens are changing. We, as student pastors, are growing and changing as we learn more about ministry from God's Word. Change is everywhere, which is why it is important that we hold on to the never-changing truth of God, "who does not change like shifting shadows" (James 1:17).

This book is about change—changing the current model of student ministry to a biblical framework. Arnold Bennett once said, "Any change, even a change for the better, is always accompanied by drawbacks and discomforts."[1] You know as well as I do that people resist change, even if it is God-honoring. Driving on the road of change can be smooth, or you can hit every pothole, and much of it depends on your steering. The questions this chapter will answer deal with change. We will specifically answer the following questions that were e-mailed to us:

> I have been asked many times, "How did you transition into this framework for ministry?" I can't help but smile and respond that I am still in transition.

- What are the potential difficulties to look for in transitioning toward a parent-based ministry, and what were the most difficult challenges you faced in moving toward this model?
- What about students from broken homes, single parents, or unchurched homes where there is not parental involvement?

This chapter will focus on facing and overcoming other

obstacles to change. Some are easier to overcome than others, and some can only be overcome by a supernatural work of the Holy Spirit. It is impossible for me to guess which obstacles you will face; you may face many or you may face few. It is also just as impossible to tell you the best way to overcome obstacles in your ministry setting; that will be up to you and the Holy Spirit as He guides you through change. This chapter will look at six obstacles you might face during this transition and what you may do to overcome them. The specific obstacles we will address are:

- Traditional Student Pastors
- Disengaged Parents
- Student Pastors' Age
- Parental Misconceptions
- Our Biblical Understanding
- The Numbers Game

TRADITIONAL STUDENT PASTORS

You might find it interesting that I started with this obstacle. I started with this one because it may be the toughest one to overcome. Most student pastors think they are anything but traditionalists, viewing themselves more as renegades and cutting-edge trendsetters. Many strive to stay current with culture, teen lingo, trendy clothes, and popular music, but the truth is, when it comes to student ministry, student pastors are shackled to the same approach that has been around since the sixties and seventies. As difficult as it is to believe, many continue to cling to the current traditional model regardless of its long-term effects on their students and their own personal families.

It's ironic but today you are considered a non-traditional student pastor if you are striving for a biblical framework and if you aren't satisfied with the results from today's model. These non-traditionalists are the brave souls who are stepping out of what has become the norm and are leading with biblical conviction rather than with trends and the latest fads. It's not hard for these people to see how out of step with mainstream student ministry they've become. It's as easy as opening the mail or visiting a Christian bookstore. If you want help in keeping up with the culture, or designing the coolest T-shirts, or launching a trendy website, or stocking up on the most up-to-the-minute music, there are plenty of parachurch orga-

> Many strive to stay current with culture, teen lingo, trendy clothes, and popular music, but the truth is, when it comes to student ministry, student pastors are shackled to the same approach that has been around since the sixties and seventies.

nizations and resources around. However, try to find a good resource that shows parents how to teach the Bible. Try to find a conference that will teach parents how to disciple their children. While it may appear odd, you are not likely to find help and will probably face some opposition in mainstream, traditional student ministry, which views parents, in many cases, as the problem.

The following are some questions that might indicate you have become stuck in student ministry tradition:

- Do you have sufficient time to lead your ministry, or is the student ministry machine running you?
- Is the lasting fruit of discipleship a main priority, or are you constantly planning your next event?
- Do comments like "We've never done it like that" or "The way we do it here is..." dictate your ministry direction more than biblical principles?
- Are your key objectives booking the coolest worship bands and hippest speakers and looking to pop culture to relate to your students? On the other hand, are your primary objectives prayer, biblical faithfulness, and simplicity?
- Do you feel more like an administrator than a pastor?
- Do the church leadership, the church parents, and others view you as the primary spiritual developer of students, or is that responsibility clearly the parents'?
- Do the parents who are involved in your ministry have a clear strategy to disciple their children?

It is difficult to break away from a multimillion-dollar student ministry mainstream. It is difficult to quit a student ministry model that most people in churches, including church leadership, have embraced and never questioned. This requires patience, courage, continual teaching and re-teaching, and lots of understanding.

DISENGAGED PARENTS

What about kids whose parents don't participate? What about single parents? What about the kids whose parents aren't walking with the Lord? We all have these teens in our ministries. We all want to make them feel welcomed and see these students grow to full maturity in Christ. If we move to a ministry mind-set that involves parents so heavily, wouldn't these students feel uncomfortable? I have had these same concerns as a student pastor. These are legitimate questions and ones that can be dealt with through biblical principles.

I continue to be questioned about this obstacle as I share the principles in this book with countless parents, pastors, and others. It seems that the traditional model of student ministry has become so engrained in our minds that we think a frame-work that closely involves parents could never work, and we think that today's broken model is the only answer. So, let's deal with the question straight on: Is the traditional student ministry model really the solution to disengaged parents?

We have covered the alarming facts about our students graduating from God in record numbers. These studies prove that when parents are not engaged, youth pastors are not effective in discipling teens because parents are the primary influencers of their children. A model without involved parents fails our students around two-thirds of the time. The model also fails families, when we see over half of all Christian marriages ending in divorce.[2] I don't see how the traditional model of student ministry is helping students or their families, and I don't see it recognizing the authority and influence God has given to parents.

The traditional model is failing our teens and families, it is not biblical, and in my opinion it is not a viable option to reaching out to disengaged families.

You may say, "Well, I just work with teenagers." If you love those teens, then you cannot leave the primary influencers out of the equation. We cannot turn our backs on the parents who will shape the teen's future like no one else. I can't accept a future of churches filled with single-parent kids, broken homes, disengaged parents, and dysfunctional families. The traditional model is failing our teens and families; it is not biblical; and in my opinion it is not a viable option to reaching out to disengaged families.

I believe that returning parents to their biblical roles and intentionally training and equipping them to complete their tasks is the best option. Following are three truths that have guided us through this obstacle. They are based on three foundational truths we believe about teens and families: they are crying out for love and care, truth to build their lives on, and a model to follow.

1. A biblical model includes a strategic plan of love and care.

Sometimes when guys share the concerns mentioned above with me I ask them, "What strategy do you have in place to minister more effectively to the needs of students whose parents don't attend?" No one has had an intentional plan in place to show me. The question about how to reach out to teens whose parents don't attend is a problem we all have, not just those of us trying to transition to a biblical framework.

We must develop an intentional plan to reach out to teens with unchurched parents and show them love and care. These students will one day be husbands, wives, mothers, and fathers. They will more than likely remain in these roles much longer than they will remain in our student ministry. Sometimes I wonder if we think our goal is to produce professional youth group attendees. Is it our role to prepare them for adulthood, for Christian marriage, and for biblical parenting? Yes, and the best way to do so is to ensure the students are around Christian homes that are irresistibly winsome.

Bridge 57 is the program for sixth graders, who are just entering our student ministry. All Bridge 57 events are father/son, mother/daughter, etc. They are designed to help parents understand we do not offer a spiritual drop-off service and to begin engaging them in ministering to their students. But how do we minister to students who don't have parents who want to attend? First, we never stop trying to reach the parents. We continually invite the parents to participate in hopes that they will be won to Christ. We make sure our Bridge 57 events are non-threatening to an unbelieving parent—paintball, date nights, overnight trips, etc. Also, these events are intentional in design to help us identify the disengaged parents very early in the ministry. If parents will not attend, adults from Sunday Bible study or small groups can step in. They can attend activities with the students and hopefully provide love and care and start relationships that can flourish for years to come. For children with only one parent who attends (whether it is a single parent or a family with only one believing parent), we work hand-in-hand with them. We haven't seen a teen boy who is embarrassed to have his favorite youth volunteer show up to play paintball with him, even if his dad doesn't come. He just wants to be loved, so we do that. The goal is to provide love and care, especially in the lives of teens with only one parent or two disengaged parents.

2. A biblical model is based on principles that you can build your life on.

When we think for a moment that we have a better plan than God's ultimate design, we are in trouble. We could never envision a framework for student ministry that is more complete than a biblical one. However, we often do just that when considering the unchurched or spiritually immature parents of our teens. We quickly discount the biblical framework of parents being the primary disciplers when a few moms and dads don't do their job. The biggest problem with this thinking is that we limit God. We say, "But you don't know our parents; they just aren't capable" or "Why try? The parents at our church think it's my job." That is in effect saying, "God's plan just won't work." The Bible is clear; parents are the primary disciplers. The Bible is powerful. When we present God's truth in a God-honoring way, His Word will not return void. It is God's job to work in the hearts of parents and teens; it is our job to align our ministries with the plan He lays out in His Word.

> We withhold the truth these students desperately need to hear because we assume they will be uncomfortable.

Sometimes we are uncomfortable in presenting the truth of how families are supposed to function because we don't want teens from non-Christian homes to be offended or feel uncomfortable. This is ridiculous when you think about it. We withhold the truth these students desperately need to hear because we assume they will be uncomfortable. Students without Christian parents need to hear teaching on the family even more than those from godly homes. In my experience, these teens hunger for the truth of how a family should work and very much want to be around these kinds of families. We must be faithful to God's framework for the family in the truths we teach as well as His framework for ministry in the ways we program.

3. A biblical model provides models for these students to follow.

If there is ever a group of students who need a model for what a Christian marriage and home looks like, it is these students. Let's not assume that these students' comfort in our ministries is more important than what they learn and see modeled from us regarding the institution of family. If the truth be known, probably one of the facets of our ministry that appeals most to these students is what they see in the "Christian home." It is so different than what they experience every day. Let's also not believe that they will figure out how to lead a Christian home some day through osmosis. We need a very deliberate plan to ensure these students are connected to homes with godly men and women.

A small group, in-home Bible study ministry, like Refinery, is the perfect forum to demonstrate to teens from non-Christian homes a different model to follow. Bible studies can point to the biblical model for families and teach what godly relationships look like.[3] Some churches also may offer mentors to these students. There are several ways to overcome the obstacle of modeling a biblical framework to teens, and you may be able to think of better ones for your ministry setting. The key is to understand this is a problem for every church, and we all must be intentional about providing love and care, truth to build lives on, and godly models for students without Christian parents.

STUDENT PASTORS' AGE

I understand the emotional gymnastics that younger student pastors have been experiencing as they read these pages. I certainly identify with the fear and intimidation they feel as they prepare to lead, teach, and equip adults older than they are, especially when many of their interactions have been tenuous or confrontational. I remember what that was like. I remember saying, "I don't even have kids; why would they listen to me?" and thinking, "Once I'm in my thirties or forties, maybe I can then start equipping parents."

The guys I feel for the most are the young student pastors who don't know when to say no and the ones who haven't had enough life experience to admonish parents who want to give up their biblical assignment. There will be a day for each of these young student pastors, and veterans alike, when parents will come and seek to abdicate their responsibility to them. Although it may not be that blatant, the day will come. What will the student pastor say on that day? Will he stand up and take advantage of the opportunity? Will he present biblical truth, or will he puff up because he thinks that they need him or that they recognize his giftedness? If you find yourself in that position, I would encourage you to know the biblical principles of the verses listed in Chapter 3 and be ready to present biblical truth in a winsome way.

I am encouraged when I see guys coming out of college

and seminary who seek to serve under pastors who will mentor and sharpen them before they lead a ministry by themselves. I have seen guys leave paid ministry positions for volunteer ones, just so they could be mentored and prepared. Think about the thirty years Jesus spent preparing for His public ministry. Think about 1 Timothy 3:10, which tells us first to test people before they are put in a position of service. Sadly, preparation and patience are not common in churches. Instead, churches want someone young so they can better "relate to the students." Another reason is that oftentimes hiring an older person with a family is more expensive. I'm not saying that a young guy can't do the job, but I am saying that a church shouldn't hire a younger pastor without a strategic plan to train and mentor him. I truly believe the leading causes of the increasingly shorter student pastor tenures is due to guys being hired too young, not having proper support and training, and being assigned a responsibility that was never biblically given to them.

If you are a young student pastor, let me say that I remember the place at which you currently find yourself. Let me also give you a few pieces of advice:

1. Pray and dig into the Word.

Become a student of what the Bible has to say concerning your ministry. Once you are convinced of His framework for ministry, start walking in His truth even if you don't have all the answers. As I have sought to be faithful in very small ways, God has given me greater depth of insight for the next step and phase of ministry.

2. Don't wait until you are forty to wake up and realize things aren't working.

Find a mentor that has been doing ministry for a while and learn from him. A mentor is someone who has been where you have not been, seen what you have not seen, and done what you have not done. Your effectiveness in ministry will be greatly improved by finding the right mentor.

3. Recruit parents who will help lead your ministry to parents.

God has been so faithful to me through the years to always provide the right adults. If you don't have the process mapped out and a perfect place ready for them, then invite them to pray, learn, and dream alongside you. I promise that you will be amazed at their input and perspective.

4. If you do not have a Parent Leadership Team, start one immediately.

Lean on team members, delegate to them, pray with them, serve with them, ask for their perspective, grow with them, and lead them. Meeting with my PLT is a refreshing, enjoyable, and enlightening time I always look forward to. I'm convinced that if anything happens to me, our student ministry would continue and prosper with such a godly, committed group of parents already in place serving with my staff. A group like the PLT

will add depth and wisdom to your ministry like no
other group can.

PARENTAL MISCONCEPTIONS

A Youth Ministry Summit was held in Texas in 2006 to
address the "mass exodus of young people from churches."
An eight-person panel made some important observations.
They agreed that the model of student ministry from which
we are operating doesn't fit the Deuteronomy 6 framework
and that we need to rethink what we are doing. Brad Bun-
ting, one of the event organizers, said, "Pastors must avoid
viewing themselves as shepherds of the adults only and be
active in leading the entire flock while encouraging parents
to be the primary spiritual mentors to their children."[4] He
continued to say, "Pastors must train the church to think biblically about what the youth ministry should be."[5] Person
after person, researcher after researcher, student pastor after
student pastor is awakening to the fact that we have lost a
biblical understanding for what we do.

Student pastors are often too busy, have too little biblical understanding, or are too new in the ministry to rethink
what they are doing. Therefore, we keep the same broken
ministry model going. Too often we don't lead from biblical conviction. We listen to parents who mean well but don't
understand their biblically assigned duty, and we listen to
accepted student ministry wisdom that doesn't deliver what
it promises.

We've all talked to or worked with parents who wanted
to hand over their responsibility to us, but they almost never

come right out and say that. They make different statements, many of which you have probably heard in the past weeks and months. We often hear statements like:

- **"You should spend more time with our kids."**
  This sounds reasonable on the surface, but it can point to a misunderstanding of what our role is. A few years ago, a dad made this demand of a volunteer on my team. I suggested the volunteer call the dad back and ask this question: "While I am spending all my time with your children, would you spend time with my children who I would be neglecting?" The point is, according to the Bible, being there all the time is the parent's calling, not that of someone else.

- **"You need to be my kid's hero."**
  Here's one we've all heard. Yes, we want to be biblical models for teenagers, but our hope is to champion the parents. They are the heroes, not us. We are in the students' lives for a few years, but parents will be there long term for their children, grandchildren, and future generations. If I am going to present anyone as a hero, it will be mom and dad, not myself.

- **"You should be at all our kid's sporting events, band competitions, choir concerts, recognition services, lunches, Bible studies, youth events, special occasions, birthdays, graduations..."** (You get the point.)
  Then they also tell us, "Make sure you aren't neglecting your own family. That wouldn't be healthy." I would guess if you are a student pastor, you aren't laughing at

this one. Our staff tries to attend students' events, but
our calling is to "prepare God's people for works of
service" (Ephesians 4:12). The parents' calling is to be
there as young people walk through the daily experiences of life: as they sit at home, walk along the road,
lie down and get up (Deuteronomy 6:7). Once again, a
statement like the one above sounds reasonable, but it
can point to a lack of biblical understanding.

- **"You should be the first person my child requests
during a crisis."**
Why would a parent ever make this statement? Better
yet, why are we flattered when this happens? No one
should be better prepared to console and comfort their
child than a parent. There are times when a professional
counselor or outside help may be needed. Then, by all
means be there or refer someone to a professional. For
the common struggles of life, however, we must champion the parents and point teens back to mom and dad
in tough times.

The toughest aspect of these statements is that they appear when we least expect them. The phone will ring in the
middle of family dinner. A parent will stop you as you walk
through the lobby after the service. We must be prepared at
any moment to winsomely present a balanced framework for
ministry and a biblical understanding. It sounds like 2 Timothy 4:2 to me: "Preach the Word; be prepared in season and
out of season; correct, rebuke and encourage—with great

patience and careful instruction." The only way to overcome this obstacle is through faithfully studying the Word and teaching it to our people. If this is a problem and you feel like you can't articulate a biblical framework, become a student of the scriptural framework for ministry to teens and parents. Point those with questions to these verses and admonish with biblical understanding and love.

OUR BIBLICAL UNDERSTANDING

Many of us have bought into the lie. We have bought into faulty reasoning that tells us today's parents are apathetic and unwilling to engage in spiritually developing their children. I can honestly say that I have met very few parents who don't care about the spiritual health of their child. Most are ready to roll up their sleeves; they just need help and direction.

One student pastor asked me, "What if our parents don't want to or refuse to accept this responsibility?" Before the Lord, they really do not have that option, unless I missed an exception clause or read a bad translation. God intends for men and women to marry and have children and teach, mentor and disciple those children. This biblical model isn't ours to adjust, improve, or ignore. We must continue to hold up truth regardless of its popularity and regardless if a few refuse to accept it. It is God's framework. We must expect Christian parents to be obedient to it.

Most parents who think their job ends as they drop off their children at the student ministry door think this way for two reasons: 1) we have taught them this convenient ministry logic and 2) we have given them the option to be uninvolved. We have created the system we now are trying to change, and we must accept much of the responsibility for the problems in today's traditional model. It is time to point out these misconceptions of parental duties. Surprisingly, I haven't met as much resistance in this area as I thought I would. Most parents readily accept their position of responsibility when I sit down with them, discuss the biblical model, and encourage them to be the primary disciplers. Why is that? It's written on their hearts. When we hear the biblical case for parents to teach their children and for pastors to encourage and equip those parents, it usually resounds in our spirits because we know it is truth. Deuteronomy 30:11, 14 gives us the principle of things being written on our hearts, saying, "Now what I am commanding you today is not too difficult for you or beyond your reach. No, the word is very near you; it is in your mouth and in your heart so you may obey it." I don't often see resistance from parents refusing to follow clearly presented truth. I would dare say that most of the resistance we meet in the area of misconceptions is due to lack of teaching on our part.

Parents ask me occasionally to help find a mentor for their son or daughter. They are delighted and surprised when

> Our role isn't to make people happy or feel good. Our goal is to encourage and equip others to walk in truth.

I immediately tell them I have a perfect match. I have asked many to read Deuteronomy 6, and I unashamedly tell them that they are the ones to play the primary role. God has placed on them a high calling to be the daily mentor of a young person. They are the first string. They are God's chosen. Sometimes I meet parents who are doing this already and just want to have someone else come alongside them reinforcing their efforts. If this is the case, I'm glad to help them find another mentor who will first partner with the parents and then will partner with their child. However, if they are looking for someone to fill the role for them, I refuse to help them abdicate their responsibility.

You may think, "If I said this, parents would get mad." Good! I get mad as well. God gave us the emotion of anger because it can lead to great results. Many times I have been presented with the truth in God's Word, and I became upset and even angry. Trust me; I want to help parents as much as anyone, but our role isn't to make people happy or feel good. Our goal is to encourage and equip others to walk in truth.

THE NUMBERS GAME

This obstacle is a serious one. I have seen student pastors get excited about rethinking student ministry, only to run into a brick wall with church leadership. Let me be clear: not all church leaders who question a change are doing so with negative motives. Most church leaders aren't familiar with the research that has recently been completed. Many have been taught to focus on numbers and aren't aware of the overall trend of decreasing baptisms and increasing numbers of students graduating from God. In Chapter 4, we addressed the crucial prerequisite of bringing other church leadership on board (senior minister, elders, deacons, etc.). Their support is crucial, or your obstacle may become a roadblock. There are very few ways you can overcome church leadership who is into the numbers game and refuses to rethink the way student ministry is done. Prayer and patience may be your only recourse. Not to be pessimistic, but sometimes this obstacle can't be overcome.

I recommend facing this obstacle with more numbers. This means up-to-date statistics combined with a biblical framework. Tell them about the majority of students who leave church after graduation. Share with them the historical numbers of baptisms and how ineffectively we are reaching this generation. If we are forced to play the numbers game in our churches, let me suggest a few other numbers to start tracking.

- **Pre-graduation student retention**
When I consider research of how many students are leaving the church after graduation, I often wonder if studies have determined how many we lose before graduation. I have not located any, but I do know that in most churches the exodus begins before graduation. Most churches experience a significant drop-off after the ninth or tenth grade. What's worse, it is accepted as "just the way it goes" in our churches. "Well you know

how it is once they hit high school... You know how it is once they start dating and driving." When we say these things, we are admitting we haven't taught our children to fear and reverence Christ above all else. We haven't taught them that God is our first and most important relationship; therefore, Christianity should affect all relationships, even dating ones.

- **Your church's graduation retention**

  Maybe we don't believe all the stats the experts are throwing our way. Maybe we're hoping all the research is wrong. Here's a test to see for yourself. Gather the e-mail addresses, cell numbers, and contact information of all your twelfth graders this year. Contact them in four years. Following are a few questions you might want to ask:

1. Do you remember who I am? (If not, stop here.)
2. Has college (or work) changed your perspective on Christ?
3. Are you attending church?
4. What is the name of the church and pastor? (Need I explain?)
5. Are you in a discipleship group?
6. Are you actively sharing your faith?
7. What is one thing we could have done to help you prepare better for life and/or college?

• **Disciples**

I speak with guys all the time who tell me, "Steve, each week at my church I am graded on my Sunday School numbers. At the end of the year I am evaluated on the baptism numbers." Just for the fun of it, let's say we feel it is an important goal to help our students understand that they are the light of the world. Just for kicks, let's imagine that it is more important that our students' lives are different, that there is a badge of distinction about them. Let's imagine that people notice and are attracted to this winsome Christian lifestyle. Let's imagine that when our students are asked about their faith, they can clearly articulate their testimony and the gospel. What if this strategy is prioritized over the current model's plan of bringing your friends to church to win a prize and let the expert share Christ with your friends? What if the end result isn't a high-attendance stunt where someone shaved his head, but rather a passion to see friends discipled? No one really wants to admit it, but we have created a ministry environment in which we offer a grand prize to get students to show up, and after years in our ministries, no one can really see a difference in our students' lives. Students attend church, but they talk the same, dress the same, watch the same shows, have the same goals, and have broken and dysfunctional families just like students who don't attend church. In short, they attend but aren't disciples. Maybe we should count not those who show up but rather those who are being discipled and held account-able and who are growing and sharing their faith.

- **Parents discipling their children**
"What? You mean you would track how many parents are actually discipling their children?" Yes, I would. If you knew me at all, you would know that I am nowhere close to the legalistic type. It's not just the numbers that interest me; I am more interested in creating an environment that helps spur parents on and resources and encourages them. As a parent myself, I know I need this type of environment. I need ideas, and I need encouragement. Therefore, we need to begin counting the right numbers, to find out who is teaching the Bible at home and who isn't. Then we must find out why those who aren't teaching the Word at home aren't do-ing so. Do they need resources, or training, or a model to follow? We won't know if we don't ask some tough questions and take an honest look at the right numbers.

I certainly haven't gotten to the point of the *Westmin-ster Confession: Directory for Family Worship,* 1647, which says,

He is to be gravely and sadly reproved by the session [that is, the elders]; after which reproof, if he be found still to neglect Family-worship, let him be, for his obsti-nacy in such an offence, suspended and debarred from

> the Lord's supper, as being justly esteemed unworthy to communicate therein, till he amend.[6]

I can't imagine a church bringing discipline on a parent who isn't teaching the Bible to their children, but I would like to see churches across America place a greater value on training parents to mentor their children. I have never talked to a parent who didn't want to do a better job. Most of the time, they are convinced of what Scripture says and want help on how to do it.

We need to change the numbers we are tracking and make sure the gauge of our success is where it needs to be.

IT'S TIME FOR A CHANGE

A. C. Benson once said, "Readjusting is a painful process, but most of us need it at one time or another."[7] Change is anything but easy. As we have described, there are obstacles and possibly even roadblocks in store for you, which begs a question: Is it worth it? Is breaking with student ministry tradition, is the time spent convincing and equipping parents, is facing tough questions from church leadership worth it? That you'll have to decide for yourself. Personally, I am fully convinced it is. Why? Because souls are at stake.

Relevant magazine published an article called "Faith No More" about the alarming numbers of young people leaving the church. The author cites research that indicates 61 percent of people who were involved in church during their student ministry years "completely disengage" in their twenties.[8] The article lists the problems as being the mentality of "Superbowl-like events" and "one-size-fits-all discipleship." David Kinnaman states in the article,

> A problem with a lot of churches is that we just have a fixation with attendees rather than disciples. Youth groups, whether they care to admit this or not, fall into that same track; if we can get more butts in the seats, we must be doing something right. And yet discipleship is a very individualized proposition.[9]

This article, like so many others cited in this book, tells us that something has to be done. Let's be honest: the research we now have doesn't point to a lot of options from which to choose. We can continue thinking the way we've been thinking and keep doing what we're doing, but we would have to be satisfied with the results we are getting from today's broken model. I'm not. I can't accept these results, and I can't follow a model that confuses the biblical roles of parents and church. It's time for a change.

NOTES

1 Taken from thinkexist.com/quotations/change.

2 Both of these facts have been amply documented in previous chapters.

3 For a teen Bible study resource that reinforces this principle, check out *Hidden Treasure* available at www.inquest.org.

4 Taken from an article by Jerry Pierce, "Youth ministry summit to explore mass exodus of young from churches," (Nov. 7, 2006) found at www.sbtexas.com/default.asp?action=article&aid=3313&issue=11/7/2006.

5 Ibid.

6 *The Directory for Family Worship* (annotated ed.; Greenville, S.C.: Greenville Presbyterian Theological Seminary, 1994) p.2.

7 Arthur Christopher Benson, taken from brainyquote.com.

8 Jesse Carey, "Faith No More. Why Are so Many Twentysomethings Leaving Their Faith?" *Relevant* magazine. Issue 24. January/February 2007, pp.50-52.

9 Ibid.

CHAPTER 8

reViSiON:

A New

Perspective

We've seen the research. We've looked at the biblical principles. We've talked about values, principles, ideas, transitions, obstacles, and more. To end our discussion, I'd like to share three thoughts with you—three thoughts about why I am glad we made the transition to a biblical framework for ministry.

1. I want to impact my family for generations to come.

I wrote in my oldest son's journal one morning:

William, you are a true blessing to your mother and me. Each day with you is a

*great adventure and a blessing to be treasured. Right
now your biggest goal in life is to play on the PGA
Tour, and with the 64 you shot yesterday, you may just
make it. More than anything Mom and I want you to
invest in eternity. One day you will have a family, and
it will be your responsibility to pass Christ on in our
family. There will be great victories, battles, failures
and many adventures along the way. Pass on the faith,
my son. "What will it profit a man if he gains the whole
world and forfeits his soul?" (Matthew 16:26). I am
sure that you are going to be an incredible spiritual
leader for your family one day.*
– Love, Dad

I want desperately for Sara, William, and Tyler to love
Jesus Christ for a lifetime. It's worth journaling to them; it's
worth passage trips; it's worth turning off the TV and having
family worship; it's worth Tina and me accepting the responsibility we have been given. It's all worth it.

I love our middle school and high school pastors; they
are two of the best out there, but I would never give to them
my role to disciple my children. I would never give up my responsibility to model Christianity and present God's truth to
my kids. I would never hand over the opportunity to impact
my family. I want to see my family impacted for centuries to
come, which is why I accept my role as primary discipler of
my children and why I want others to do the same.

2. It's exciting to be a part of something that is contagious.

I hope one day you experience how contagious God's framework for discipleship can be. In recent years our church has created an environment to encourage parents to think of creative ways to be primary disciplers of their children. Here's what I mean:

- One father in our ministry prays over his boys every time they leave the house. It isn't long or drawn out, but he simply puts a hand on them or hugs each of them and prays that God's blessing will follow his boys that day. Recently his oldest, who is away at college, was home visiting, and as he was about to leave, he said, "Dad, I'm leaving. Aren't you going to pray God's blessing on me?"

- I have a dad in my ministry who is a man's man. He is the kind of guy who doesn't show emotion—the kind who never cries. He is John Wayne and Clint Eastwood rolled into one, but I know a secret about him. He does indeed show emotion, and he cries often now. His wife told me that after his children are in bed he opens the Passage 7 Journal we gave him and before he is ever able to write one word to his daughter he weeps.

- There is a couple in our ministry who has recently been reading the Bible with their children. It really is a pretty simple plan. When they come together, this husband and wife ask their children if any of them have a question about what they read. The children are asking spiritual questions, and they are studying God's Word together at home.

• One mom in our ministry wanted her son to have a thirteenth birthday he'd never forget. She asked everyone who had a spiritual influence on her son to write a letter of encouragement to him. On his birthday, he received this special book of personalized letters that respected influencers had written specifically to him. Talk about a gift of legacy.

• Another friend of mine wanted to encourage his son and asked the influencers in his son's life to help him with a Journey Day. His son spent his birthday working through a scavenger hunt that led him to each of the influencers who individually taught him a very valuable lesson and gave him a gift to help him remember the lesson taught. When he returned home, the men were all there, and this young man had to tell all of the men what he learned that day about being a godly man.

• Two of the biggest hunters in our church both have girls and no boys. Each year they load up their girls, sit in deer stands, and talk for hours with those precious girls. These girls have great confidence, and they know their dads love them (and they also know more about deer hunting than most of the boys in our ministry). When these girls look for a husband one day, you can bet they will know what a godly man is supposed to look like.

• One dad refused to accept the typical father/daughter

relationship drift that he saw coming on, so he came up with a plan. His daughter mentioned once that she had a desire to scuba dive. So, each week he loaded up the family and they went for lessons so they could get certified. One summer they drove to Key West, and that young girl had the week of her life. To this day their relationship remains strong.

- Another dad in our ministry started a journal for each of his three children before they were born. When his three children turn eighteen he plans to present these gifts of love to each of his God-given treasures. He says each time he writes he is reminded of his responsibility as a dad and asks God to help him.

- I recently received an e-mail from a dad who was in Thailand with his oldest daughter. Next year he will be taking his middle child to Turkey for that child's personal mission trip. He takes each of his kids on mission trips because he and his wife so desperately want their children to know that the world needs to know the Lord and that Christ's plan for the world includes them.

- A few months ago a dad was checking his laptop, and the history revealed that his son had visited a few unapproved sites. The student was ashamed and broken when his father confronted him. The next morning the dad took the son to breakfast and renewed his role of protector and defender for his son and established an accountability plan and strategy to help his son. His son is now working within this framework and thanks his dad for his loving and deliberate response.

- Another family established "Daddy Days." Once a year, dad takes each one of the kids on a trip to do an activity together one-on-one, usually overnight or longer. The reasoning was to allow for extended, uninterrupted time together to talk about things going on in the child's life and the child's relationship with God.

- One dad and son meet weekly to share prayer requests and go through one chapter of Proverbs together after reading and studying it separately. They are intentional about building a godly relationship with each other that will last a lifetime.

- One mom used the time driving her kids to school to disciple them. They would read from Max Lucado's daily devotion, and the kids took turns reading. She spent the time applying the truths to her children's lives and spiritually preparing them for the day at school.

- Another mom and dad also drove their kids to school until they were juniors or seniors. Every day they drove them to school together and spent time praying for their protection, their health, their mind, and their opportunities to share Jesus with others as well as for God to help them do their best at school.

- One dad is writing journals for each of his three children. The books include memorable events they've had together including the times each prayed to receive Christ, fun times fishing and camping, and other favorite memories. The journals will be his personal gifts to each of them at the rehearsal dinners of their weddings.

- One mom and daughter taught Sunday School together for a year. According to the mom, they still remember how special that year was as well as the lessons they learned about commitment, being on time, responsibility, etc.

- Another mom sent her husband and boys away on a trip as she and her daughter did a makeover on the daugher's bedroom. That weekend was spent discussing what it means to leave childhood behind and become a godly woman. The mom says that it was a powerful bonding experience.

- One family challenges their children to read through the Bible. As the children are younger, they read through simpler children's Bibles. After they read through one, they are taken on a special event and presented with a more challenging Bible. Some of the children read through five Bibles before they graduated high school.

These stories could go on and on. The point is that this kind of thinking is contagious. Parents begin continually thinking of creative ways to keep the relationships with their teens strong and intentionally protect their role as primary disciplers. There is enthusiasm in our ministry when we hear about parents being daily mentors to their children. There is anticipation to see what new ideas will surface next. There is an excitement in our ministry that is contagious, and I am thankful to be a part of it.

3. I want to invest my life into something that is lasting.

I believe this can be said of every student pastor I have met. As I began asking tough questions about student ministry and questioning if my ministry produced lasting fruits, I quickly discovered that something had to change.

Several of my closest friends are student pastors in their forties and fifties. One can't make it that long in student ministry without some serious soul searching. Not one of these men has told me he is pleased with the results student ministry is producing. They know something has to change and so do I. We are all determined to rethink what we are doing and make sure the ministries we are leading are grounded in God's Word and producing lasting results.

I recently attended a funeral of a gentleman who died at the age of fifty. For the last eleven years of his life, Jim was trapped by muscular sclerosis and was confined to a nursing home, but he never stopped ministering. His funeral was packed, and there were testimonies after testimonies of his spiritual impact. His wife and children love Christ. People groups on several continents now have God's written Word in their language, and several thousand know Christ because of his mission work. He wasn't busy playing games although he always had a good time. He wasn't too busy as an administrator to disciple his children and other new believers. One day I will take my last breath, and I want to be found faithful just like Jim. I want to serve God in something bigger than myself, something lasting.

It scares me to think how busy we have become, especially when the research clearly shows us that our busyness is producing little fruit. If we aren't careful, if we don't rethink what we are doing, we can work hard for years and rarely see "fruit that will last." I want my ministry to be different. I want my life to yield eternal results. I am determined to rethink student ministry and find ways to impact families for generations, and I am convinced that lasting impact can only come from reestablishing a biblical framework for student ministry.

> If we aren't careful, if we don't rethink what we are doing, we can work hard for years and rarely see "fruit that will last."

DECIDE FOR YOURSELF

This book is written to allow you to decide for yourself. It's your call. You may think it's not trendy or flashy, or even that it's old-school, to put parents back in their place as primary disciplers. (I'd question that logic, since I see no loopholes in the biblical passages listed in these pages.) You may think that a change may not be worth the time, trouble, and tears it may cost you. You may look at the leadership in your church and believe they won't support you. You may think it is a great concept but you aren't equipped to pull it off. You'll have to decide for yourself: Is it worth it?

When I see parents take seriously their role as primary

disciplers, I'm reminded that it is worth it. When I see a mom take her daughter on a transition trip and discuss purity with her, I'm reminded that it is worth it. When I see a disengaged dad come to a ministry event with his son for the first time ever, I'm reminded that it is worth it. Rethinking student ministry is hard. Breaking with student ministry tradition is daunting. Change takes time, prayer, and hard work, but I believe it is all worth it.

I've made up my mind. I refuse to settle for two-thirds of our students graduating from God. I refuse to accept half of the Christian marriages in my church ending in divorce. I refuse to be happy with ministry based on gimmicks, hype, and trends that fade. I've decided to rethink what we are doing, to ask some tough questions, and to search God's Word for its framework of ministry.

It's your turn. Will you rethink student ministry? Decide for yourself

ABOUT THE AUTHORS

Steve Wright and his wife Tina are the primary disciplers of their three teenage children: Sara, William, and Tyler. He lives in Raleigh, North Carolina, where he also serves as Pastor of Student Ministries at Providence Baptist Church. Steve grew up in Gainesville, Georgia, and has served as a student pastor for more than twenty years. He is a graduate of Carson-Newman College and New Orleans Baptist Theological Seminary. He also founded InQuest Ministries out of his desire to equip and serve student pastors. InQuest produces Sunday School curriculum and discipleship resources used in churches worldwide.

Chris Graves and his wife Anne are the primary disciplers of their two young sons: Wyatt and Rex. He lives in Corydon, Indiana, where he also serves as Student Pastor at First Capital Christian Church and as a writer for InQuest Ministries. He is a graduate of Carson-Newman College and Southeastern Baptist Theological Seminary.

OTHER RESOURCES AVAILABLE

ApParent Privilege

Parents have the greatest privilege of their lives in front of them every day: raising their children. Pointing their children to Christ, modeling the gospel, and talking about God's grace shouldn't be a burden. It is a privilege. *ApParent Privilege* provides biblical understanding and up-to-the-minute research to encourage parents in the unparalleled opportunity they have to be the primary influencer of their children. This book presents parents with a biblical framework for parenting within both the family and the church. Put this book in the hands of parents to better equip them to pass on a legacy of faith to their children.

HELP! I'm a Minister's Wife!

Author Tina Wright combines 134 survey responses and her fourteen years of experience as a minister's wife to present an honest, probing look into the lives of women serving alongside their husbands in ministry. Issues addressed include criticism, loneliness, expectations, genuine friendships, and meeting husbands' needs. *Help! I'm a Minister's Wife!* is a book designed to encourage your wife in her role as well as strengthen your marriage and ministry.

Visit **www.inquest.org** to order these resources.

Check out Steve's Blog at http://lastingdivergence.com
Lasting Divergence provides resources and encouragement for pastors seeking to equip parents.